THE LEADERSHIP LIBRARY
V O L U M E   1 8
CALLED INTO CRISIS

Other books in THE LEADERSHIP LIBRARY

Well-Intentioned Dragons by Marshall Shelley

Liberating the Leader's Prayer Life by Terry Muck

Clergy Couples in Crisis by Dean Merrill

When It's Time to Move by Paul D. Robbins, ed.

Learning to Lead by Fred Smith

What Every Pastor Needs to Know about Music, Youth, and Education
by Garth Bolinder, Tom McKee, and John Cionca

Helping Those Who Don't Want Help by Marshall Shelley

Preaching to Convince by James D. Berkley, ed.

When to Take a Risk by Terry Muck

Weddings, Funerals, and Special Events
by Eugene Peterson, Calvin Miller, and others

Making the Most of Mistakes by James D. Berkley

Leaders by Harold Myra, ed.

Being Holy, Being Human, by Jay Kesler

Secrets of Staying Power by Kevin A. Miller

The Magnetic Fellowship by Larry K. Weeden, ed.

The Healthy, Hectic Home by Marshall Shelley

The Contemplative Pastor by Eugene H. Peterson

THE LEADERSHIP LIBRARY

Volume

18

Called into Crisis

The Nine Greatest Challenges of Pastoral Care

James D. Berkley

Carol Stream, Illinois

WORD PUBLISHING

Dallas · London · Sydney · Singapore

CALLED INTO CRISIS

A Leadership/Word Book. Copublished by Christianity Today, Inc., and Word, Inc. Distributed by Word Books.

Cover art by Joe Van Severen

Though the case histories that appear in this book are used with permission, names and identifying details may have been changed in some cases to preserve the privacy of the parties involved.

Library of Congress Cataloging-in-Publication Data

Berkley, James D., 1950-

Called into crisis : the nine greatest challenges of pastoral care / James D. Berkley.
    p.   cm. — (The Leadership library : v. 18)
       ISBN 0-917463-23-4 : $10.95
       1. Pastoral counseling.   2. Clergy—Office   I. Title.
II. Series
BV4012.2.B38   1989
253—dc19   89-570
                                           CIP

Printed in the United States of America

9801239 AGF 987654321

In memory of my father,
Donald William Berkley
(1911–1980),
who by his capable handling
of life's calm and crisis
gave me a rich example of how our
heavenly Father carries us through crises.

CONTENTS

INTRODUCTION
PASTOR, HELP!

The call into crisis may be in the middle of the night or in the middle of a meeting. It may come from active church members or from active church avoiders. It may result from something that makes you worry or that makes you weary. Or even wary.

That doesn't matter. To the parish pastor, the cry of distress will come. Inevitably. Repeatedly. Discomfortingly. People need someone — right now! — and pastors, with hope and a prayer, respond.

They drive off into the night to accompany a father and his teenage son to the emergency room to pump a stomach filled with prescription drugs. And they'll be there the next day as the weary family tries to put family life back together.

They dash to the golf course and arrive concurrently with the new widow, rushing — too late — to see her husband who has collapsed in the noonday sun. They touch her shoulder as she gently picks fine grass clippings from his hair and smoothes his collar just before the ambulance drivers roll him off on his final trip.

Pastors gather their courage and ring a doorbell, wondering if it will be heard over the cacophony of rage from a marriage turned violent. Two who once vowed to love and cherish are about to hit and run, and it's the pastor who's called to enter the home and alter the outcome.

So, filled with a mixture of dread and desire, half wanting to be in another state yet knowing God wants them right there doing his work, pastors step into all kinds of crises. Most do it regularly. Most do it courageously. But none do it effortlessly.

Just how do pastors get involved in so many disturbing circumstances? It comes with the position. Pastors are called into crisis.

The original call comes from God, for the call into ministry, itself, is a call into the chaos of the fallen world. If Christians' lives were all tightly wrapped into neat, passionless packages devoid of surprises or tragedies, pastors would have little to do but sip tea with the insipid.

But Christians aren't sheltered from life's realities. Until the age to come arrives, and Christians' problems evaporate like a bad dream, the primary guides through difficult times will be the leaders of God's community. Certainly pastors answer a call into crisis when they take on the care of people in a fallen world.

But the call into crisis becomes much more tangible when it arrives in the form of a jangling telephone at 4 A.M. or a hopeless sob outside the study door or a desperate whisper in the narthex. God isn't the only one calling pastors into crisis. Parishioners' crises of body and spirit call forth pastors' care.

But do pastors feel prepared? Capable? Fit for the task?

After all, who's really fit to piece together a shattered marriage? Who's prepared to call on the father whose .44 magnum in his daughter's hand snuffed her flickering flame? Who's sufficient for the questions an agonizing adolescent seeks about his homosexuality?

Yet pastors respond and care for the hurting of our world — despite their misgivings, despite their frailties, despite the fact that things don't always work out spectacularly.

But they would like to be as effective as possible. Hence *Called into Crisis*. The lessons of experience can guide the crisis responses of tomorrow — or the next hour. Pastors can learn from those who have been there, who've ministered when called into crisis.

The Nine Toughest Pastoral-Care Crises

Pastors find themselves called into a number of crises: problems with kids, loss of a job, arrest, rape — you name it. People get in binds, and pastors get involved. So many, in fact, are the kinds of crisis-care situations, a single volume could never contain them.

To limit the scope to a reasonable number, the editors of LEADERSHIP Journal, in conjunction with the research department of Christianity Today, Inc., surveyed clergy subscribers of LEADERSHIP to find the most difficult pastoral-care crises commonly faced.

Of nearly 450 surveys received by pastors, 103 were returned, a 23 percent response rate. Using the tallies from both fill-in questions and forced-choice scales, we found nine crises that pastors considered both difficult and frequent. The nine, in descending order of perceived difficulty, are: domestic violence/family abuse, suicide, homosexuality, death of a child, drug/alcohol abuse, divorce, adultery/sexual misconduct, death of a spouse, and catastrophic or terminal illness.

(A tenth crisis, congregational personality conflicts, scored high in difficulty and highest in the time spent on it, but since that crisis usually involves the pastor, it wasn't included.)

Chapters 3 through 11 each cover one of the nine greatest challenges of pastoral care, with extended stories, insights, principles, and a list of resources for further reference. The Quickscan sections at the end of each chapter are designed to be useful immediately in a crisis situation. The table of contents lists the Quickscan section for each category of crisis.

But I suggest reading and digesting the entire book before placing it an armspan from the phone. Information gleaned from one chapter may come in handy in another kind of crisis — and we can never know too much about how to attack the next crisis we are called into.

Assumptions

In writing this book, I've made a number of assumptions. The first: I am no master counselor. I have, however, taken great pains to find those who, by training and experience, are excellent crisis counselors. They represent a broad spectrum of denominations and backgrounds, and it is their wise counsel I've gathered and distilled into this book.

The second assumption is that most of you aren't full-time, professional counselors. I assume you're pastors, busy a good part of the week preparing sermons, putting together church programs, and wondering why you ever consented to chaperone the junior high lock-in. You want to give good measure to those in crisis, but time constraints force you to work smart rather than long. Your counseling has to fit within a typical pastor's typically out-of-whack schedule.

Third, I assume you already know the basics of counseling. You've become accustomed to a style that fits your personality and theology. This book is meant to provide specific insight and help for situations that may still make you tremble, although you've had to handle them by necessity.

Fourth, you care deeply about people. They aren't your customers; they're God's children entrusted to your care. You love them. You feel for them. You want to help them.

Finally, I assume you bring the strength of the gospel to bear on crises. You are not just any people helper; you are an agent of the Living God armed with the power of the Holy Spirit. Yours is not merely a secular role; you represent God and his people. The peace you seek for your counselees is more than a lack of crisis; you want them to know God's *shalom*.

ONE

CRISIS

No counsel is more trustworthy than that which is given upon ships that are in peril.

LEONARDO DA VINCI

I fell into someone's crisis by default. Newly ordained as an assistant pastor, I was sitting in my leather chair in my expansive office feeling rather pastoral when my intercom buzzed. "Jim, I've got someone on the phone who wants to talk to Toby. Do you want to take the call?"

"What's it about?"

"She won't say. When I told her Toby had gone to another church, she just asked for any pastor. I think I recognize the voice. She called Toby sporadically for a number of months."

"Thanks. Put her on." I tried not to sound too eager.

The voice on the other end of the line came across drained and hesitant: "Hello? Uh, are you a minister?"

"Yes I am," I replied, trying to sound as competent as my new title and office would have one believe. "My name's Jim. What's yours?"

"I better not tell you. But you can call me Cory. That's what I told Toby."

"Well, Cory," I said smoothly, leaning back in my chair the way I'd seen executives do on TV, "what can I do for you?"

"I don't know. I don't think anybody can do anything for

me anymore. I'm not even sure — I probably shouldn't be wasting your time." It sounded like she was going to hang up.

"Wait a minute, Cory!" By now I was sitting up straight. This wasn't going as I'd expected. "What do you mean 'wasting my time'? That's what I'm here for. I want to help. Tell me what's going on."

"Okay," she said after a long pause. "Look, I'm feeling pretty worthless right now, and I didn't know where to turn. My parents kicked me out of the house. They told me I can't be their kid anymore."

"I'm sorry to hear that," I said, honest emotion showing in my voice. "Why would they do that?"

"It's a long story. You probably wouldn't want to hear it."

"No, tell me. I want to know."

"Well, promise you won't tell anyone?"

"Of course, Cory, not without your permission."

"It's important, because if word gets out that I've talked with you, my parents are gonna be mad. Well, anyway, before I was born my mother had a little thing going with a delivery man, and that's how I came about. My dad's a big lawyer in town; I can't give you his name, but he comes to your church sometimes. Well, he and my mom had a terrible time about me. When I was a kid, they sent me off twice to live in foster homes. I guess my 'dear' mom couldn't bear the sight of me — reminded her of her big mistake. But both times they eventually took me back. I was back home through high school. I did really well. Got a scholarship to college. I really tried to do everything to please them, because I didn't know why they'd sent me away. But everything seemed to be going okay finally. Now, this summer, it all falls apart. A couple of weeks ago out of the blue they kicked me out again. Just like that!"

I was stunned. "Cory," I said, "what did they say?" There must be more to the story.

"They told me, 'You're a great kid, Cory, but it just isn't working out having you as our daughter. You're going to have to leave. It's time for you to be grown-up and just accept the fact that you have to be on your own now.' You know, they didn't even have the guts to tell me the real reason. I had to get it out of my brother the other night. But that night I thought I'd shock them, so I told them, 'Okay. I'll move out tonight.' "

"What did they do then?" I asked.

"They helped me pack."

All I could think of saying was, "Cory, I'm so sorry!" By now I was leaning intently over my desk. I'd thought this would be a routine troubled-teenager case. I was a youth director; should be a piece of cake. But this was something else. I searched for how to respond. "How are you getting along now?"

"Not very good. Look, I just want them to take me back! Aren't kids supposed to be loved by their parents?" The last statements were spoken with pathetic vigor. "If they don't take me back, I don't know *what* I'll do!"

"Whoa, Cory! What are you telling me? This sounds pretty serious." *Am I hearing veiled suicide warnings?* "How about us getting together to talk? You could come to the church, or I could meet you somewhere. Where do you live?"

That final question bothered Cory, and she backed off. She'd already revealed too much. Her voice turned distant, wary. "Why do you want to know?"

"Hey, I just want to help, and I can't help if you don't let me." *Jim, you're losing it!* I thought.

"Uh, I've got to go now," Cory broke in unconvincingly. "It was probably a mistake to call. You've got better things to do than talk to losers."

"Wait, Cory! That's not true."

"Well, I've got to go. I may call you back later."

Just before she hung up, I got in a final word: "Call me anytime, Cory. I care abou — " Dial tone.

As I sat there, I felt anything but pastoral. *A crisis call — this girl needs help! — and you can't even keep her on the line. It's a good thing Dr. Bower wasn't grading you on that one!* BERKLEY FLUNKS CRISIS COUNSELING — *I can see it now.*

That was my first crisis call in my first pastorate. A couple of counseling sessions, and I expected Cory to be back in the loving arms of her family. And I'd feel good about myself and my validity as a pastor.

The crisis may have belonged to Cory, but I had become wrapped in it. Part of the attachment came because of my call into God's helping profession, but part of it involved my need to be significant and show genuine human compassion. As time went on, and I matured in ministry, I began to sort those two intertwined motivations. Cory gave me a lot of opportunity.

A Strung-Out Crisis

Cory did call back — several times in that first week. In those subsequent calls, she warily parceled out bits of information about herself: she worked in a shop downtown, but she wouldn't give the name; she lived nearby, probably in a residential hotel; she had no phone number, or wouldn't give it to me; she described her parents as snooty, heartless socialites more concerned about appearances than her; her brother's wife had just had a baby, and Cory feared she would never be considered the aunt or even see the baby.

One call followed an incident with her mother. Cory had dropped by to see her, but the mother had gotten mad. As Cory put it, "She was enraged about what the neighbors would think seeing me drop by dressed as I was. I just wanted to see her. I suppose I wanted some sign that she loved me. But she thought I wanted money, so she dug into her purse and handed me some. I was so embarrassed and ashamed."

Cory had called me out of that shame: "What kind of person am I that they want to push me out of sight?"

Another day she called me after lunch. She was obviously distressed. She said she had been talking with her father. Then, quickly, she hung up. She called back later, but I was tied up. She then called me at home in the early evening, but again was hesitant to talk. She had to retain control, it seemed. One part of her desperately needed help; another part couldn't stand becoming vulnerable, getting close to anybody. Finally, she called later. Need had conquered pride. We talked ninety minutes.

"Jim," she said, "I got really sick last night. I didn't know who to call, but I had to talk to somebody. So in desperation I called my dad and told him, 'Dad, I've *got* to talk with you.' I must have sounded desperate, because he came to my place — all dressed up in his three-piece suit.

"Then I made a real mistake. I guess I just fell apart — started crying and all. Dad can't stand that. He never could take emotion. So he began to shake me and tell me to shape up. I got hysterical and finally screamed at him, 'I hate you!' That really made him mad, and he started shaking me violently, and then he slapped me."

I was shocked. "Cory, he shouldn't have done that!"

"Well, he did. Maybe I deserved it. I walked across the room and leaned against the wall. I couldn't believe this was happening. I just sort of slid down the wall to the floor, covering my face with my hands. I cried for a long time. When I finally looked up, Dad was standing at the door, one hand on the doorknob and the other angrily on his hip. Know what he said?"

"What?"

"My own dad — he said, 'You've got to handle this yourself. I hope you have enough self-respect not to go running to someone for help.' I guess I believed him. I probably shouldn't be telling you this now."

She went on to say how her sickness wasn't any better and she was worried. She was utterly hopeless, beyond any expectation of reconciliation.

I begged her to tell me where she was so I could pick her up. "Cory, you've got to let Debbie [my wife] and me help you! Let us come get you and bring you here. You need help; don't play games with us." She nearly capitulated, but eventually her defenses went up again. No, it wasn't going to happen. Not that night. Not for some time.

Two days later she called again; she had to initiate the calls since she hadn't so much as divulged a phone number where I could reach her. It's 2:30 in the afternoon. She's really sick. She's afraid. I offer to take her to the hospital, and she almost goes. She sounds desperate. Then she abruptly breaks off the call.

Thirty minutes later she again calls. Again, she won't let me take her to the hospital, although she's scared to death. She fears her father will find out she went to the hospital and be ashamed of her. By this time, *I'm* getting desperate. She hangs up.

Now it's 11:15 P.M. Cory is calling collect from twenty-five miles away. She's nearly hysterical and often breaks down into sobs. Evidently she has committed some petty crime, but she's frustratingly vague about it. *Her blasted control!* She's terribly shaken, scared, alone, remorseful. Doesn't know where she is, doesn't have her coat or shoes, doesn't have a shred of hope — and will not cave in to our pleas to let us get her! After a half hour of wrenching conversation, Cory says, "I love you and Debbie" and hangs up abruptly.

I hung up the phone and cried. And prayed. That, and telling her we cared for her, too, was all I could do.

Over the next several days I received a number of calls from Cory. She was okay again, she said. Now she was living in the wilds, literally under a tree not far from a highway. She got phone money by cashing in bottles she found. Sometimes we just chatted like friends. Other times she sounded petulant and petty, turning on me, accusing me of not caring, sounding hard and independent — "I don't care anymore. I can take care of myself!"

She told of another minister nearby who tried to help her but gave up on her when she wouldn't take money for food or a room. She felt she had failed in yet another relationship and wasn't sure she'd ever succeed again. "If you give up on me," she said solemnly, "I don't know what I'd do." Her control again. But yet it *was* understandable.

I tried once early on to talk about faith. Perhaps rather clumsily I spoke of God's unconditional love, how he never forsakes his children. But she became almost mean in response. "I don't want to talk about God ever again," she muttered, rather bitterly. "It's easy to talk about love when everybody loves you, but that's not for me, so don't ever bring up that stuff again, okay?"

I decided to be honest with her. "That hurt me, Cory. When I talk about God, it isn't just words. There's nothing more real to me than God's love. And he loves *you*. I don't want to go along giving you little handfuls of sawdust when my pockets are full of gold." She seemed sorry after that, but I didn't push the subject. I did tell her, however, that I'd leave my porch light on until she decided to come to our house — just like God does.

One time she said, "I'm getting weary with life. I'm not sure why I go on. What's there for me to live for? Nobody wants me. Wouldn't it be better if I just ended it all?"

I went into the suicide-prevention mode. "Do you know what you're saying? Are you serious about it? I want you to know a lot of people care about you."

"Oh, I'm not the suicide type," she replied, almost jauntily. "My father has given me too much pride and strength to do something foolish like that."

The next evening at 8:30 Cory phoned. "Your porch light is off," she announced. It was the first time in a week I'd forgotten to have it on.

"You won't believe this," I confessed, "but it really has been on every other night. Where are you?"

"I'm down the hill at McDonald's — but don't come down. I just wanted to drop some things by your house."

This time she was too close to let out of our grasp. After some nimble talking, I finally convinced her to let me meet her in the parking lot. Out behind the dumpster, sitting on concrete tire stops, we talked for ninety minutes. Then I coaxed her into coming to the house to meet Debbie. A half block from the house she panicked: "Stop the car; I want to get out. Debbie doesn't want to see me. I look awful." I finally convinced her to go to our house, but our conversation took place outside. She wouldn't go inside. She insisted on giving us two large chocolate bars and three dollars "for the collect calls." A half hour later, we stood under the porch light and watched her walk into the night.

Cory approached and walked away at odd intervals for the next eighteen months. We got cards and calls from Orange County, Washington State, Los Angeles, nearby towns. She aimed to get back into college, but she had neither the money nor the emotional energy to do it. For a time she'd be in an apartment or hold down a job. Then chronic health problems or another wave of misery would push her back into the street.

We gave her small amounts of money from time to time. We called, wrote when we could. Once she stayed a couple of days in our home. We told her over and over that she mattered to us. We did talk to her about God, and she began to respond. One day — unbelievably, just when I thought life was coming together for her — her fiancé died in a car accident. I had to help break the news to her.

The last time I saw Cory was in a Burbank hospital. As the culmination of a number of serious physical ailments, Cory had contracted what we thought was amyotrophic lateral sclerosis — Lou Gehrig's disease. She was blind — temporarily, we hoped — but in reasonably good spirits in the hospital room. She'd come a long way in piecing life back together. She knew Christ and the love of his people, but her medical prognosis looked shaky at best.

My final entry in her file read: "4 / 7 / 77: Cory's now blind and deaf. 'There are two important things in life,' she told me, 'to be honest with somebody, and to know somebody loves you.' "

I didn't see her again. She gave no forwarding address, and I didn't know her real name.

The Heart of a Crisis

At the heart of any crisis, as I learned vividly those months, is someone who has lost control.

One analogy is driving an automobile. Put us on a winding mountain road or a spaghetti-like interstate interchange, and we expect to be able to handle it. When a deer darts suddenly into the road, without thinking we swerve or put on the brakes. The vast majority of times our learned mechanisms work, and we go on down the road feeling a little relieved but quite in control of our circumstances.

But other times something causes us to lose control. Take ice, for example. As a 16-year-old I braked to stop at a perfectly flat intersection — and our '56 Chevy ignored my frantic corrections and veered diagonally into the curb. I'd hit a sheet of what Washingtonians call *black ice.*

The Chevy sustained no damage, but my sense of the orderliness and predictability of driving did. I learned that sometimes there is *nothing* you can do. All the routine coping mechanisms fail; the car is out of control. It's an awful feeling.

It's akin to what people in crisis experience. They know life brings difficult turns and unexpected hazards, but so far, they've found ways to steer their way out of them. But then comes the black ice. The brakes, their means of gaining control, don't work, and their lives bash into a brutal curb.

At this point, when their coping mechanisms have been expended to no avail, people are in crisis. Life has gone out of control. They need help.

Such was the case with Cory. How can a child grow up with any sense of self-worth or basic security when she is shuttled in and out of her home at the whim of a disturbed mother? And then, just when life seems to be coalescing, just when her self-conscious pleasing behavior seems to be accounting her "worthy" to be included permanently in the family, she's booted out and told to grow up — and not show any disgusting weakness.

Cory had obviously gathered some coping mechanisms before this final blow. She was an intelligent, capable girl. She had also learned to manipulate people, playing the game of "kick me" to see how much they really cared. That backfired on her when her parents helped her pack the night she tried to shock them.

She'd learned to be wary with people: If you open up and become vulnerable, you just may be rejected, so maybe it's best to pretend to reject them before they have a chance to shaft you. She liked to control emotional distance. She longed for closeness but would back away before others would have what she perceived as leverage on her.

Cory also had an amazing strength and resilience. She reminded me of my childhood "Roľy Poly," an egg-shaped toy weighted in the bottom: someone could punch it and knock it over, but it would always right itself.

But none of these coping mechanisms was enough when her parents shoved her onto emotional black ice. She hit a crisis point — several times — and that's when my phone would call me into crisis.

The Components of Crisis

Many factors in a crisis either help or hinder a counselee's ability to scramble out of it. One way to look at these is to ask a series of questions.

Is this crisis caused by real or imagined factors? In one way, this question is irrelevant, because it's a bona fide crisis when someone *perceives* he's in crisis, whether or not that perception has any basis in reality.

Albert Ellis, the sometimes controversial proponent of rational-emotive therapy, postulates that our perceptions of events affect our behavior more than the events themselves.

In fact, our feelings aren't products of the event; they're products of what we tell ourselves about the event.

For instance, I had a class reunion last summer. I told myself it ought to be fun to see friends and reminisce about high school. Therefore, good emotions; no crisis. But what if I had put on seventy-five pounds and just been released from jail? The reunion would be the same event, but I might tell myself, *You're a failure. If you go, everybody is going to be shocked at how you've turned out. But if you don't go, people will think the worst.* That perception — what I tell myself about the event — could well provoke a crisis.

This helps explain why an event that hardly touches one individual may knock another for a loop. Much depends on the inner interpretation the person gives the event. Understanding this, we know not to make light of anyone's crisis. What may seem routine to us can be deadly serious to another.

That's why it's wise to determine what the counselee is saying to himself or herself about the event. When a counselee's fiancé dies, it would be easy to think, *This young woman's dealing with grief.* But behind that single event may be a woman who's lost another fiancé, or who wanted to break off the engagement, or who was driving the car in which her fiancé died. If so, she'll be telling herself different things about the death.

Beginning to understand those volumes of self-talk can help a counselor deal with either the precipitating event or the perceptions of it, true or skewed.

What history does the person bring into this crisis? Since no crisis is an isolated life event, what people bring into the crisis has great bearing on how they survive it. Some people are simply more equipped than others to plow through personal crises. I was amused by a desk plaque that read: I CAN HANDLE JUST ABOUT ANYTHING BUT ADVERSITY.

Who is most prone to cope poorly? In his book *Crisis Counseling,* H. Norman Wright lists several characteristics of those

NB who have trouble handling crises: (1) people already hurting and emotionally weak, (2) people in poor physical condition, (3) people adept at denying reality, (4) addictive people with oral fixations (drinking, smoking, eating, or talking excessively), (5) people with poor conception of time and timing, (6) those who struggle with excessive guilt, (7) people quick to assign blame to others, and (8) the very dependent or independent.

To that list can be added a ninth characteristic: people without faith or with immature faith. The religious can sometimes fall apart as easily as the atheistic. But a deep and abiding faith in the sovereignty of God and the unchanging love of Jesus Christ can be seen only as an asset for long-term crisis resolution. Such people maintain the sense of God being in control despite temporary evidence to the contrary. They hold out for the wide-angle picture of the meaning of events. Perhaps crises help separate those who say they believe from those who *believe*.

To understand someone's crisis means looking beyond the immediate disaster into the course of events and experiences that got the person there.

What support does the person have? It's murder to go through a crisis alone. Often the social support the person receives spells the difference between positive crisis resolution and long-term disastrous effects.

To again use Cory as an example, family had pushed her out, and she had shed friends. Had she not "disobeyed" her father's wishes and sought a string of pastors and counselors in her wanderings, her crisis would have been the death of her.

The person with a strong network of family and friends can bear much more stress than one taking the assaults of life solo. That's where the church can make such an impact as it fulfills the role of family for those who have none.

What symptoms are present? When a person feels incapable of handling the situation, we may see many of the following symptoms, Wright suggests: headaches, vomiting, hyperventilation, fainting, depression, panic, sleeplessness, or bleeding ulcers; a feeling of being absolutely overwhelmed, beaten down, defeated; the desperate, often frantic, need for rescue or relief ("You gotta help me!"); and a general shut-down of abilities when all else is jettisoned to focus on the crisis.

At times the symptoms become the crisis, such as when a desperate person attempts suicide as one way to "make the hurting stop." Then all attention obviously is focused on the symptom. The rest of the time, the symptoms point pastors to the underlying problem, which will go on producing a string of symptoms until it is treated. Pastors offer appropriate care for acute symptoms, but they want most of all to trace the symptom trail to the source.

The Pastor as Participant

Pastors bring themselves, their faith, and a number of inter-personal tools into crisis intervention. The trick is to become involved in a therapeutic way, one that neither tries to take the crisis from the counselee nor remains detached and aloof from the very present human need.

Looking back at my initial contacts with Cory, I see now how my need for validation as a "real minister" was at play. New in the ballgame, I wanted to show I could field adroitly whatever came my way. Any pastor who counsels must fight the urge to do it for personal benefit. The need to be needed runs strong in most people, and counseling can offer wonder-ful ego strokes.

The desire to become overly involved flows especially high in crisis counseling. Few pastoral coups compare to jumping into someone's mess and effecting a dramatic solution. We'd like to be able to stuff such victories and hang them on our study walls. But we can't.

What's "too involved"? Assuming responsibilities the counselee is capable of handling. Shielding the counselee from behavior consequences he or she needs to feel the full impact of. Helping to perpetuate a lie. Each of these actions can harm the counselee and impede crisis resolution. The pastor is there to help, but too much help can become tyranny.

One California pastor said, "I've got to remember just whose problem it is. It's not my problem to keep, so if people try to hand it to me, I just hand it back and say, 'It's yours. How can I help you with it?' "

The following chapter focuses on general crisis intervention before we launch into the nine chapters on particular crises.

TWO

HANDLING A CRISIS

Toward men and toward God, she maintained a respectful attitude, lightened by the belief that in a crisis she could deal adequately with either of them.

ROBERT NATHAN

Every crisis is different. That means there's no single way to help someone through one. There are, however, some tested approaches. Let's look first at a framework for the counseling process, and then the theological underpinnings for crisis intervention.

The Stages of Counseling

Gerard Egan, in *The Skilled Helper*, spells out in layman's language a manageable and practical course of events for counseling that makes a team of the helper and the one in need. Egan's scheme divides counseling into three stages — problem definition, goal development, and action — each of which he further divides into three steps.

Egan wants helpers to remember who is the central figure in each stage of the helping process. He feels "clients should 'own' as much of the helping process as possible. The steps of this model are actually tasks the clients need to accomplish, with the help of counselors."

Stage I: Problem Definition. The job at this stage is to uncover the nature and dimensions of the crisis. We can be of no help if we don't know what's wrong.

In crisis counseling, determining this may be done more quickly than in more routine situations. Problem definition may be sketchy as you pull on a coat and hurry out the door, but at least you want to know if the person you're rushing to help is more apt to commit suicide or adultery.

• *Step I-A: Helping clients tell their stories.* In crisis situations, it's not always easy to get people to talk — or to talk coherently. Shock, trauma, anguish, emotion — many things contribute to the difficulty of getting the story. Some people say little, others so much that you don't know where to begin.

The first assessments are made at this step by both the pastor and the person needing help. The pastor is beginning to put together an accurate picture of the needs. The person in crisis will need to understand that picture soon, but first is busy assessing the helper: Does she have the skill to help me? Does he look like he knows what he's doing? Can I depend on her?

Trust must be built on the spot in many cases. Often it's based on your appearance, body language, physical presence, and command of the situation. Sometimes a relationship exists, but the crisis often adds a dimension that has to be negotiated with skill.

The task at this step is to facilitate the telling of what has happened and is happening, to get information on the table. A pastor may need to draw out one person, separate another from a distracting situation, or calm another.

Charles Shepson provides an example of this kind of sensitivity. Shepson, founder of Fairhaven Ministries, a counseling and retreat center in Roan Mountain, Tennessee, finds people often break down in tears when they call with a problem. If someone starts crying, he'll say gently, "Go ahead and cry as long as you want. You won't hear me saying anything, but I'll be praying for you. We can talk some more whenever you feel ready." With that thoughtful response, he spares them embarrassment — and gives them the sense he's handled situations like this before and knows what he's doing.

• *Step I-B:Focusing.* This step involves screening, focusing, and clarifying.

Many clues present themselves to the helper: bits of stray conversation, things the helper sees, information given by others, conversations with the counselee. The pastor needs to perform a kind of information triage to decide what really is being said, and the person in crisis needs to determine what to talk about. This is screening.

When an alcoholic comes to a pastor for help, his problems may involve a crumbling marriage, a job on the rocks, acute health problems, legal entanglements, financial difficulties, depression. Not every one of those problems can be handled at once, and not all of them contribute equally to the crisis. The pastor and alcoholic need to determine which problem demands first attention. Criteria such as perceived importance, apparent solvability, the relative pain it is causing, and the counselee's willingness to work on it all help determine where to begin. And that's focusing.

Clarifying is the process of probing a problem to add to one's understanding of it. Exactly how bad is the alcoholism? When did it start? How does it affect life?

● Step I-C: Blind spots and new perspectives. Parts of the crisis may not be known or recognized even by the one in the crisis. Everyone has blind spots, and a crisis can exacerbate them. The alcoholic may think the whole crisis revolves around his messed-up marriage. An accident victim may be crying about a smashed car, not realizing a sore wrist is actually broken. A homosexual may think that recovering from an assault is his major need.

On the positive side, new perspectives can provide the first glimmer of hope for those in crisis. A counselor may help the alcoholic consider the effect his alcoholism has on every other part of life. The homosexual may be led to believe for the first time that there's hope for his greater healing. Sometimes counselees need to be challenged to look at things a different way, to own their problems, to look for a way to change their situation. This final step of the first stage prepares the way for stage two.

Stage II: Goal Development. In this stage, the counselee, having understood the problem, starts to imagine what he'd like to replace that problem. Egan writes, "Counseling is successful only to the degree that it leads to problem-managing action." In other words, in Stage I the problem is identified and clarified, but most people don't want a clear problem; they want a solved problem. That's why Stage II leads toward beginning to solve the problem.

● *Step II-A: Constructing a new scenario.* No one wants to remain in crisis. However, it's possible to go from the frying pan into the fire. Drowning in alcohol the loss of a child may temporarily make the parent forget, but it brings on a worse crisis. Counselees need to think about which direction is up.

Egan calls that activity constructing a new scenario: "A new scenario is not a wild-eyed, idealistic state of affairs, but rather a conceptualization of what the situation would be like if improvements were made." This scenario becomes the goal.

For instance, getting arrested for indecent exposure forces a man to realize that he needs help. In talking with his pastor he may construct a scenario with two elements: the ability to live without succumbing to hurtful urges and a life without a sense of constant shame. He isn't envisioning never to be tempted, nor does he expect Miss America as a companion. He is looking toward a reasonable and obtainable future.

● *Step II-B: Critiquing the new scenario.* This step makes the counselee look closely at the newly envisioned scenarios. Will they work? Are they obtainable in a reasonable amount of time? Which one is most realistic? If I could have only one, which would it be?

Pastor Gary Gulbranson of Glen Ellyn (Illinois) Bible Church devised a unique way to help a young woman look at new scenarios. The woman was hospitalized after almost overdosing on laxatives. At the hospital she took too many sleeping pills and nearly died. Her major problem appeared to be anorexia and bulimia, but Gary realized the roots of her problem went deeper.

To help her, Gary gathered key people in her life: a boyfriend, her parents, two roommates, and church members she was close to. Together they conferred with her about her problems and broke them down into smaller, manageable parts such as her binge eating, her problem relating with people, her lack of employment. Each of the seven people agreed to work with her on one of those problem areas. The church also paid her way to a treatment program. With that kind of creative help, the woman had several ways to improve.

"Goals, if they are to be translated into action," Egan writes, "need to be clear, specific, realistic, adequately related to the problem situation, in keeping with the client's values, and capable of being accomplished within a reasonable time frame." A parent who has lost a child to suicide would have to throw out a goal "to have everything as it was." It's unrealistic. Likewise, a goal "to feel better" needs to be more specific. "To be able to appreciate the happy times we had, unhindered by remorse" is a good goal.

Counselees then need to consider the consequences of the choices they will make. This isn't always easy for the pastor to enable or the counselee to do. Sometimes painful choices will have to be made — temporarily leaving an abusive spouse, telling an employer of a drug dependency, deciding to end futile efforts to maintain a child's life. Even considering the choices is not easy, much less making them, which is the next step.

● *Step II-C: Choice and commitment.* This final step of Stage II may demand more than some counselees feel able to give. An alcoholic often balks at this point. A suicidal person may feel unwilling or emotionally unable to choose to live. While pastors cannot choose for the person in crisis, they can make the choice easier. Egan lists several ways that choosing and commitment are made easier. For instance, clear and detailed scenarios give greater incentive than fuzzy ones; several options give greater incentive than just one; harder, more substantial, goals are actually more motivating than small plans.

In this step counselees need care and support in order to make tough decisions.

Stage III: Action. Once people know what the problem is and have an idea where they want to head to get out of it, they can move toward the preferred scenario. It's a long way from wanting to do something, though, and accomplishing it. That makes this stage so important.

- *Step III-A: Discovering strategies for action.* In a way, it's brainstorming. Suppose a new widow feels paralyzed with the prospect of managing her financial affairs. She realizes that her grief centers around her fear of going it alone. She envisions herself able to manage the checkbook and make investment decisions that won't damage the nest egg her husband and she had accumulated. How is she going to get there?

Her list might include reading books on personal finance from the library, getting her daughter to show her how to do the books, hiring a financial consultant to advise her, paying for someone to keep her books, taking a class at the senior citizens' center. Getting the widow to explore these options, and even come up with more, is one way to motivate her to work through this aspect of her grief in a productive way.

Go for a number of possibilities, says Egan: "Coming up with as many ways of achieving a goal as possible increases the probability that one of them or a combination of several will suit the resources of a particular client."

- *Step III-B: Choosing strategies and devising a plan of action.* With the various strategies on the table, pastor and counselee collaborate to decide which course of action best meets the counselee's needs, fits his or her values, and seems likely to succeed.

The widow mentioned above may decide she doesn't want to burden her daughter and can't afford professional help. So she decides to get some library books, talk to her friends, and, if necessary, give the class a try. These strategies fit her mood and her sensibilities.

So next she needs to set up a plan: When will she check out the books? Who among her friends will she ask for advice, and how? Where is that senior citizens' center, and when do they offer the class? If she can break down her larger decision into smaller steps, she finds she can accomplish her decision. Putting the mini-steps into a realistic time frame keeps her moving toward her goal: I'll go to the library on Friday, and by Tuesday, I want to have the first book skimmed.

It's important at this point, and throughout the process, that the plans be the counselee's. The pastor wants to encourage and support, but only the person in crisis can do what is necessary to move beyond that crisis, which is the final step.

● *Step III-C: Action.* Eventually the rubber must meet the road. It won't necessarily be a smooth trip, and pastors are wise to stick close by to offer help and encouragement.

If a good plan was formulated in the previous step, obstacles and ways around them were probably anticipated. Still, Murphy's Law enters into crisis counseling, and probably some unforeseen setbacks will occur. If the counselee is forewarned of this possibility, he or she won't be taken by surprise.

The widow learning to manage her financial affairs may find her math rusty. Her seemingly proficient friend may be better at doing books than teaching how to do them. The class may move too quickly or too slowly, or the widow may find it embarrassing to allow someone else to see her income and expenses. But these setbacks are minor. Her plan is good, and she basically needs help over these little obstacles.

A counselor can take into mind the principal facilitating forces and restraining forces and then help the counselee work through these. Negative forces could arise from the environment (It's difficult to get to the senior center), the counselee's thinking (Burt said I'd never have to worry about these things!), imagination (Everybody here knows more than I do), or emotions (I cry whenever I see Burt's handwriting in the ledgers).

Facilitating forces are reinforcements such as a checkbook that balances, the encouragement of fellow senior citizens in the class, or the sense of accomplishment following a good investment.

It's the rare crisis case, of course, that glides through this process without some fits and starts. Some crisis cases actually end somewhere in the first stage. Once the counselee tells his story, he has the personal strength to fly through stages two and three. Some crisis situations compress the three stages into one marathon session that proves sufficient.

Pastors actually view crises differently from most helpers: they'll live with the people long after the crisis is past. They'd like to use the crisis event as a springboard for ongoing pastoral nurture and spiritual development. They want not just happy people but committed disciples of Jesus Christ. And so they add a tenth step to the process: follow-up.

This ten-part pattern can serve as a model for what usually needs to be done over the entire process of care. It allows pastor and counselee to work together systematically to alleviate a problem, but it keeps the major work of the problem where it belongs: in the hands of the person in crisis.

Counseling Theologically

Charles Lake, pastor of Community Church of Greenwood, Indiana, says, "I work out more theology in the automobile on the way home from a funeral home than I ever do in my study." Crises have a way of bringing out issues and making theological understanding of critical importance.

But what are the key theological concepts for a crisis counselor to think through?

Gary Sweeten, associate pastor of College Hill Presbyterian Church in Cincinnati, identifies four. He believes the Christian counselor has a leg up on secular counterparts because Christians understand the results of the fall: bondage, rebellion, guilt, and shame. Some counselors focus on only one of these problems, and in so doing, miss the wide spectrum of reasons for people's crises. Those with theological understanding can work on all four areas.

"Being in bondage," Sweeten writes, "implies that we are blind to our sinfulness and impotent to change those things of which we are aware. . . . we cannot, by our own works, do anything to redeem ourselves from our sinful condition."

People facing problems of homosexuality, alcoholism, or sexual addiction certainly know what Sweeten is talking about.

Rebellion involves our decisions to go against the will of God. The quip, "Sin is revolting," proves literally true. Many of the crises people face are the result of someone's rebellion against God.

Guilt is not just a feeling; it is the result of violating God's law. Whether we feel guilty or not is more a matter of how we were socialized. But when God's standards are broken, we stand condemned and guilty before God. Only confession and repentance remove the legal guilt we've accrued.

Shame is what we feel when we understand our shortcomings, and shame can ruin a life and cripple recovery. Shame says, *I am an awful person.* It's a natural consequence of a sound conscience mixed with a violation of God's standards. While confession breaks the hold of guilt, it may not ease shame. People need the understanding of their new position in Christ as God's child to rid themselves of the shame occasioned by the Fall.

The theologically astute counselor can attack problems in all four areas. For instance, a drug addict has reached a place of bondage to drugs. He cannot free himself. He got there partially by acts of rebellion. He stands guilty of that rebellion, and, if his conscience isn't seared, he feels shame for his actions. Attack only the rebellion, and the very real aspect of bondage sabotages the efforts. Deal only with the shame, and the guilt remains. Work through all four aspects, and you can end up with a person set free from bondage, rebellion, guilt, and shame.

David Seamands, professor of pastoral ministry at Asbury Theological Seminary in Wilmore, Kentucky, adds a final, fundamental area of thinking for the crisis counselor. He told me, "I want all the students who leave my classes to have worked out an adequate theological understanding of suffering. Otherwise they will be ambushed when they run into people experiencing difficult circumstances. They need to realize how God relates to this world and works through secondary causes to get through to them." Seamands wants pastors to have the theological understanding needed to undergird their work with people in crisis — including themselves.

The Desired Result

In *Crisis Counseling* H. Norman Wright speaks of Jesus walking the road to Emmaus with two of his former followers, both in deep crisis following the Crucifixion. He built rapport with them by listening to them. He confronted them after a while and gave them a new reality in order to change their thinking. "Then an interesting thing happened," Wright observes. "It is something that every helper dreams of doing with some of his helpees — especially the more difficult ones. Jesus 'vanished from their sight' (v. 31)! In so doing, Jesus left them on their own and spurred them to action. This is the ultimate goal of all helping — to move the helpee to a point of independence where there is no longer any need to rely on assistance from the helper. This . . . is the crux of crisis counseling."

Perhaps we can go one step further. The ultimate result of our caring for people in crisis is to draw them to wholeness of life in Jesus Christ. They need not depend on us when we help move them beyond crisis to Christ.

For further study:
Egan, Gerard. *The Skilled Helper: A Systematic Approach to Effective Helping.* Monterey, Cal.: Brooks/Cole Publishing Company, 1986.
Kennedy, Eugene. *Crisis Counseling: The Essential Guide for Nonprofessional Counselors.* New York: Continuum, 1981.
Swihart, Judson J. and Gerald C. Richardson. *Counseling in Times of Crisis.* Waco, Tex.: Word Books, 1987.
Wright, H. Norman. *Crisis Counseling: Helping People in Crisis and Stress.* San Bernardino, Cal.: Here's Life Publishers, 1985.

THREE

MARITAL CONFLICT AND DIVORCE

*If marriages
  Are made in Heaven,
    they should be happier.*
THOMAS SOUTHERNE

Every once in a while I hear of a couple married dozens of years who "never quarreled once." I always wonder if they're amnesiacs or liars.

Place two sentient people together in marriage, and conflict is bound to occur. In measured doses, conflict can be productive; it forces growth and change, compromise and resolution. It releases tensions constructively rather than letting them build to dangerous levels.

But when does the normal jostling of any marriage relationship become a crisis? "It needs to be defined by the individuals involved," offers Ed Smelser, a counselor at Fairhaven Ministries in Roan Mountain, Tennessee. "Just as some people can handle more physical pain than others, some couples tolerate more marital discord. But a body can stand only a certain amount of pounding, and a couple can take only so much anger and quarreling. Tension is inevitable. Arguments are common. But when the situation becomes so painful that a couple can't see the marriage continuing — that's a crisis."

What is the pastor's proper response when a shaken marriage totters in near collapse — and when some do eventually topple? Here are engineering plans to shore up the tottering and rebuild the devastated.

Outsider In

While our presence in some crises will be welcomed, our very entrance into a marriage crisis is often strewn with ambiguity: They want a pastor, but they don't. Or one does, but the other resents it. It's difficult for the pastor, an outsider, to know the expected role when summoned, sometimes ever so faintly, into a marital crisis.

A marriage crisis rarely grows in complete obscurity. Signs of disintegration begin to appear around the edges of the relationship: an increase in separate activities, coldness toward one another in social situations, marital "humor" with barbs, public bickering, rumors of family fights, children who suddenly become a behavior problem or allow their grades to plummet at school, a dropoff of church involvement. Pastors notice these signs and wonder what to do.

Sometimes unwelcome messages reach the pastor: "Do you know the Schulzes are having trouble?" When the rumors prove accurate, the pastor has a decision to make: to initiate or to respond. Both tactics have pros and cons.

Initiating can make you an unwanted intruder. Therefore, many pastors wait, prayerfully, to be involved by one of the spouses. "Unless someone is willing to reach out for help, willing to change," I heard over and over as I talked to pastors, "the chances of helping that couple are nil. Somebody has to want help enough to be willing to involve you. Otherwise they may listen politely (or not so politely!) to what you say, but they'll go out and do what they'd planned to do all along." When invited, the pastor can work on problems with the support of at least one participant.

Thus it appears wise to wait until invited.

Charles Shepson, founder of Fairhaven Ministries, said, "Sometimes when I hear a former student or acquaintance is having marital troubles, I'll write to tell him I care and to offer help. The vast majority of the time I get no response. Or when I do hear back, it's usually months later, *after* things have really fallen apart or when things are safely back together.

When I've caught a couple in the midst of a crisis, they seem unable or unwilling to let me help. But when they reach out to *me*, it's another story altogether. Then I've seen a lot of good things happen."

But waiting for the drowning to call for help is a wrenching job for lifesavers. Aren't pastors supposed to care for their people, even when parishioners don't know enough to request it? Should pastors helplessly sit on their hands while marriages go under?

These difficult questions have led many pastors to adopt this philosophy: Normally I'll allow couples the dignity of asking for help. But I won't knowingly allow a marriage to disintegrate solely because no one invited me in.

The Beginning of Care

Of all people, one's spouse has the greatest opportunity to cause pain and frustration, just as that same person is most capable of giving pleasure and fulfillment. For this reason, marriage difficulties cut deeply.

When initiating pastoral contact, one of the biggest jobs will be to control and channel a range of emotions. The crisis often unfolds with one spouse unable to cope with the pain of a rocky marriage and seeking the pastor's help. A woman whose wedding I had performed about a year earlier called to ask if she could see me in my office. While settling into our chairs, she got to the point: "Keith and I aren't doing well."

"I'm sorry to hear that, Jeanne. What seems to be the matter?"

"It's probably not fair to put it this way, but it's his family. I don't think I'll ever be a part of them."

"What about them is hurting you?" I asked.

"Keith and his parents and brothers are in the trucking business together. Don't get me wrong; it's going well — maybe too well. That damn business is all any of them ever think about!"

It was the first time I'd heard her use that kind of language.

"You sound put off by the Kalahars! But every new couple has to learn how to fit into one another's families. Is there anything else?"

"It probably wouldn't be that bad for anybody else, but do you know how clannish the Kalahars are? I mean, we all live together on property right near the shop — my mother-in-law is right out my kitchen window! They're always having birthday parties and anniversaries and business celebrations. But if the party's for my side of the family, forget it! They expect Keith and me to *live* for the business, and Keith doesn't seem to mind. He does whatever the rest of the family wants. Well I don't want to be a Kalahar — at least not that much of one. I want just a little piece of Keith for myself and to do things our way."

"I can understand. Have you and Keith been upset with each other?"

"*Upset* is hardly the word for it. I didn't feel good on Tuesday, so I told Keith I didn't want to go to a party for his cousin. We had a big blowup. He accused me of trying to turn him against his family, and I was so mad by then, I told him I hated his stupid family. Then I split for my friend Carol's place. I ended up going back home that night, but Keith and I have hardly been speaking. Keith's been out of the house most of the time. But what's new about that? He cares more about his trucks than he ever did about me!"

Jeanne had a crisis: She still loved Keith, but they had a lot of things to work out. Jeanne came to me looking for help, and I wanted to see to it that the marriage God had joined together no one would put asunder. How best should I proceed?

Ed Smelser offers sound advice for pastors: "When people first come to you, they tend to describe situations to best fit their needs. Out of frustration, anger, bitterness, and hurt, they tell you everything that's wrong with the other person. I like to meet with a couple together to have them both tell their side."

Jeanne was probably telling me the truth as she knew it, but it was edited truth, a piece of the story. I'm sure Keith had plenty to fill in from his viewpoint. I had to be careful not to jump to conclusions. I needed Keith's insights and attention to do all I could for them.

"It's important to get them together also," Smelser continues, "because even sitting in front of you, they have to practice good marriage communication: letting the other person speak, letting him or her finish, not controlling the conversation. I like to observe how they relate to each other, so I 'let them go at it' to a degree. I learn a lot about them and their relationship in that initial interchange."

After an initial meeting with both parties, many counselors find it wise to meet with each person separately. Charles Shepson usually follows this routine. "The second time I meet with a couple, I try to talk with each of them alone for thirty to sixty minutes. That's a time when each can talk openly without any regard for how the other is taking what's being said. For instance, the husband may say, 'I feel almost nothing for my wife anymore.' He couldn't say that in front of his wife without hurting her, so probably it just wouldn't be said.

"The wife may say, 'I've told Bill about one lover, but actually I've had three. He'd never be able to take it if he knew how many, and especially who they were.' That's valuable information that eventually Bill needs to hear and handle, but it never would have come out had I not talked with Bill's wife in privacy. I can ask questions and get answers unimpeded by the effect those answers would have on a spouse."

"I tell them they may say anything they want about our individual session," Smelser says, "but I make a case for not talking about it outside our sessions together." When they report on their time with the counselor, they often "forget" parts embarrassing to them, misquote the counselor for their benefit, or give some misreading of what was said or done.

After he meets with the couple separately, Shepson gathers them briefly to plot their next steps. This helps discourage excessive curiosity about "What did you say about me in there?"

If a counselee doesn't talk, says Smelser, "I try to draw out that person by saying something like, 'You must have your reasons for being quiet.' Suppression of anger, or passive aggression, can be just as injurious to a marriage as active hostility."

The idea to keep in mind here is that emotions *are*. They may be acted out or stuffed deep inside, they may frighten or bewilder or dominate, but they need to be acknowledged. *Then*, they may be faced and worked on.

Shepson says, "One of my jobs is to get feelings out into a setting where they are neither judged nor discounted. I want the person to know his or her emotions have a right to exist. Later we may talk about the right and wrong actions springing from these emotions, but at the moment, I need to give permission for these emotions to be expressed."

Care Objectives

Once the couple has expressed their emotions and described the basic issues, the counselor can work on some basic objectives. Ed Smelser has five objectives for the next few sessions. These provide a marriage counseling routine in outline.

Controlled release of tension. Smelser's initial goal is to gather data in a "safe" setting. He lets the couple get things off their chests, but disallows verbal abuse and hateful statements that will later be regretted. A couple has built pressure in their relationship for a number of months or years. When they finally reach a crisis, that pressure is ready to burst out in destructive ways. Merely allowing them the dignity of being heard releases pressure.

Increased understanding of issues. Emotions cloud reasoning, and both parties likely come with a limited or distorted view of their marriage. Whether overly pessimistic, unnecessarily blameful, or excessively naive, their understanding often needs massive doses of unbiased observation.

"Have you considered . . . ?" questions help couples view their problems from a new perspective. With Jeanne, I mused, "Keith has had thirty-some years in close association with his family. I'd probably have a hard time including new ways into old habits, too. I'll bet he isn't even aware of how much his family continues to influence him." Jeanne, in her hurt, may not have had the charity or clarity even to consider that.

Communication with, rather than at, each other. The prior need, of course, is to get a couple talking _to_ each other. It's not uncommon for a counselor to hear a spouse talking as if the other weren't there: "I wish she'd just once — only once! — be on time for church!"

The natural response to that is, "Jill's here. Maybe you could say it to her."

"Oh, yeah. Uh, Jill, think you could try to be on time more often? I hate being late for meetings."

Since communication problems are at the heart of so many marital crises, simply getting the two parties talking _together_ can be a major step toward health. But the quality of that talk is important. According to Smelser, "Many of the things one person says make the other erect defenses."

The wife says, "You never think about all the things I do for you." The natural response from the husband is, "I do too! Just yesterday I thanked you for packing my lunch."

To the wife, Smelser might say, "The way you talk seems to be triggering defensiveness in your husband. If he feels you're attacking, he's going to want to defend himself. How about saying something like, 'I sure like it when you notice the things I do to keep this family going'?"

Smelser continues: "Most wives, when they say, 'Don't read the newspaper,' don't really have anything against newspaper reading. What they intend to say is, 'Talk to me!' If the husband would only talk a few minutes with his wife, he could read the paper unmolested for hours. So we have to get _N B_ people to say what they _want_, not what they don't like."

Refocusing on one's own responsibilities. By the time marital problems get out of hand, both parties have likely done a lot of brooding on what the _other's_ failures are. The wife is full of

"He doesn'ts," and the husband loaded with "She won'ts."

"The focus must be taken from 'faults I think my partner ought to work on,' " Smelser says. "I may say, 'I'm really not interested in who has the majority of problems. The issue is for each of you to say, "What am *I* doing to contribute to our problems? What can *I* work on to make things better?" ' I try to help them refocus on their own choices, on their individual responsibilities, on what they, themselves, need to know or do or say. It's in the present *doing* that the marriage is going to be saved."

Genuine appreciation for the other's feelings. "People don't have to agree," Smelser assures us, "if only they *understand* the other person's position. I want to work with a couple until each develops a genuine appreciation for the other person's position — regardless of whether he or she agrees with it. One woman said to me about her husband, 'We still don't agree, but I feel so much better just knowing he fully understands my opinion and is taking it into consideration.' "

This understanding applies not only to husband and wife but to couple and counselor. Smelser believes that "people seem to know, at some level, where their problems are and what needs to be done. But they're in crisis and feel incapable of doing anything. I've found that simply agreeing with their intuitive analysis actually helps them do what their intuition has told them is right. Also, when they get my confirmation — 'He agrees with me!' — they're accountable because I've said, 'I see what you see.' It's a lot harder for them to rationalize after that."

Separation and Divorce

Questions of separation and divorce arise with more regularity than any pastor would want. However we may feel about divorce, people come to us bleeding from its beating and in need of crisis care.

"Before students leave this seminary," says David Seamands of Asbury Theological Seminary in Wilmore, Kentucky, "I tell them they must have their theology of marriage, divorce, and remarriage worked out. If they don't, they'll find out within the first few months in the parish why it's so important."

One of the early concerns is when to advise separation. In cases of abuse (see chapter 5), nearly everybody urges separation. No one should be required to live with fear of injury. Other situations also point toward separation. Some spouses participate in illegal activities, and remaining in the same household could subject a mate to legal implications or criminal dangers. Sometimes a dominant spouse insists the other participate in immoral actions. When it comes to obeying man or God, one has to obey God — away from the control of a tyrannizing spouse.

Other situations are less clear-cut. What does one advise when two people seem to be tearing down each other, when all that's resulting from their crumbling union is destruction and pain and anger? Many suggest a trial separation to allow tempers to cool, emotions to change, and clearer heads to prevail.

Separation is not intended to be a prelude to divorce, but rather a means toward eventual reconciliation. Crisis counselors need to make clear with the couple their intentions. "I come right out and ask them, 'Why are you separating? What do you expect to gain from this move?' " says one pastor. "If they hem and haw and come up with vague answers about 'needing space' and 'wanting more freedom,' then I try to get them to be more specific. I may point out the costs of living apart, and they're substantial. I draw a mournful picture of the effect on the kids, if there are any. I don't want separation to look like a simple answer. It can so easily be a regression to immature coping mechanisms, like running away from the problem.

"But if the couple has thought through the implications, and if they're able to set up a way to continue working on their relationship while separated, separation can break a hurtful pattern. Many times I've seen couples return to marriage gladly; they don't find being apart much fun."

The separated need help coping with their new arrangements, and direction and impetus to keep working on their tottering relationship. The counseling concerns expressed earlier still apply, but with greater urgency.

Divorce sparks many wildfires in a person's life. Questions of finances, identity, sexuality, "success" as a man or woman, child raising, and living accommodations smolder beside the smoky issues of sin and guilt. Since divorce involves brokenness and sin, confession and forgiveness are in order. Divorce is not the unforgivable sin. By clarifying a person's responsibility for the sin of divorce and by "absolving" the truly repentant through prayer and pronouncements of forgiveness, many pastors have helped the divorced work through their sense of guilt.

Fortunately, the pastoral counselor is not alone. The body of Christ can help people cope with the many transitions of divorce. For some divorcees, the crisis may be as prosaic as a lawn mower that won't start when the lawn is a foot high and growing by the hour. Single parenthood, job re-entry, household maintenance, cooking, loneliness — the newly single have a rough time handling such experiences.

That's where a church can shine. In one church several men proficient with cars regularly provide safety checks, change the oil, and perform simple maintenance for the cars of single parents in their church. In other places men take the sons of divorced mothers fishing, or women help daughters of divorced fathers with hair care. In other places self-help groups like Parents without Partners meet in churches. Pastors may provide individual counsel, but church families have the ability and availability to care deeply for the divorced in their midst.

Personal Considerations

It's remarkably easy to get caught up in someone's marriage crisis. What's not easy is maintaining that delicate balance between professional distance and pastoral warmth. Many pastors say the most volatile counseling situation involves a male pastor and a woman with a troubled marriage. So easily the "thoughtful, caring pastor" can be seen as the answer for a woman with a "thoughtless, brutish lout" of a husband. And so easily the warm affirmation translates into sexual attraction. The flesh is weak.

And it's also vulnerable. It's not unknown for pastors to be intimidated by passion-torn spouses. One pastor tells the story: "One day a woman from my church asked to talk with me. She said she felt in danger from her husband. When I asked why, she said, 'He wants to get rid of me.'

"I didn't know her husband, and from the way she described him, I was glad. Apparently he'd grown fed up with her and wanted her out of his life, so he was doing incredibly mean things. He figured if he intimidated her enough, she'd just leave.

"He especially wanted her to sign over the house to him, but that would mean she'd leave without a penny of assets. I told her she didn't have to be bullied into signing anything and encouraged her to stick up for her rights. I also warned her to leave the house if he started acting dangerous.

"Not long after that her husband came to see me. He wasn't at all pleased with what I'd told his wife, and he seemed intent on changing my mind. When his six-foot-four frame came through my door, I knew I was in trouble. Pointing accusingly at my sternum, he raged, 'If *you* hadn't talked to my wife, she would've signed the papers and let me have my house!'

"I don't know what came over me, because I was scared, but I said, 'You may be over six feet tall, but you're only half a man if you're trying to take that house away from your wife.' Somehow that worked. They did divorce, but she got the house, and she lived in it for years in retirement. Although he swore there was no other woman involved, the husband married two weeks after the divorce."

Another danger: being linked too closely to one party. Ed Smelser says, "It's easy to feel closer to one person in the couple. Maybe you feel that person has a better handle on what needs to be done and is more willing to do it, or maybe the person seems to be more the victim. That can be a problem, because both persons ought to be able to expect your impartiality.

"Often the woman seems to garner special favor. Maybe it's because women are generally more sensitive to relationships. Perhaps it's a protective instinct. Whatever the cause, though, I need to remain impartial to be effective."

One cost of marriage crisis intervention caught me by surprise. Soon after I had met with Jeanne, she seemed to turn against me. She'd taken some turns for the good in her marriage, but suddenly in church matters, whatever I was for, she was against. After several months of locking horns with me, she finally announced her decision to leave the church.

I hadn't failed her as a counselor; she had been appreciative of my concern, and she appeared helped by my advice. Nor had my opinions and pastoral style changed. So why the clash?

Probably because I knew too much. She had revealed their difficulties, and my being privy to their dirt was hard for her to live with. In her awkwardness, she left the church, ostensibly over our disagreements. That is sometimes a price to be paid for crisis intervention.

Marriage crisis intervention also can be highly frustrating. I worked with one couple for nearly two years. To the husband, his wife was a cold fish with unreasonable expectations she'd never allow him even to attempt to meet. To the wife, the husband was a troubled and selfish mother's boy unable to show he really loved her.

I could see why both felt as they did. From outside the labyrinth, I could watch them bumping their way through the marriage trying to find each other. But they could see only an endless array of walls. Although I could tell what it would take for them to succeed, they were either unwilling or unable to make it happen.

In frustration and dismay, I watched them wend their way out opposite exits of the maze, unable to find and hold on to each other. Pastors, who care about people and see the awful destruction of divorce, feel the sorrow of a home divided, of children uprooted, of love turned into bitterness and self-reproach. Sometimes it hurts to be called into crisis.

It Isn't All Ache

But what keeps us going are the occasions when our intervention has impact. One missionary wife sent this testimony to her pastoral counselor following counseling:

"I felt trapped between my feelings and my Christian convictions. I hated my husband and wanted to leave him. I honestly did not know how I could go on living with him, feeling the way I did. I knew that to leave him was wrong and would have far-reaching consequences for my family. *And we were missionaries!*

"I knew what was right. I could quote all the verses, yet I had myself convinced at times that it was more cowardly to stay in the marriage than it would be to leave it. My whole life was misery. I was rejecting everything I believed in.

"My husband and I were given an opportunity to go to a Christian retreat center for counsel, and in agreeing to go, I made my first tentative choice to work on our marriage. My first day there, I made a deliberate choice to commit myself to my husband and to our marriage. It was a decision based upon what I knew to be right, but it in no way reflected my feelings at the time. I still felt rebellious and bitter. I felt no love, and these feelings stayed with me. Each positive step I took was a response to my choice as I ignored my feelings.

"We started to rebuild our marriage. Our first aim was friendship, since we felt this was a measurable, reachable goal. I had no expectations, but I stuck with it, knowing only that I was doing the right thing. My miracle happened — slowly, very slowly. As I acted on my choice and built on it, my feelings began to change. Over the months I began to feel respect, then tenderness, and finally love for my husband. I saw his weakness, and I saw his strength. I saw him through entirely different eyes, and I loved him." Success!

Quickscan
MARITAL CONFLICT AND DIVORCE

Immediate concerns:
1. Assess the potential for physical assault. Should one of the spouses leave the premises? Might you be in danger when you intervene? If so, call the police.
2. Decide whether to wait to be asked to help or to take the initiative. Waiting may make you more effective, but it can also allow a situation to move beyond redemption.

Keep in mind:
1. Emotions will be high. Expect tears and anger. Emotions need to be vented in a controlled situation.
2. Two people, and usually a vast supporting cast, have caused this conflict. Rarely is there a true villain and victim. There are normally two sides to the story, both of which need to be heard.
3. Resolution of the problem will likely be a long process. For months and years they have built to this crisis; a snap resolution seems improbable. Crisis counseling can help them move from destructive to constructive modes of relating.
4. Your role is to open lines of communication, to help the couple hear and understand each other, to "translate" misunderstood communication and draw out the unspoken.
5. As long as each person's focus is on what the *other* ought to do, the conflict will continue. When the focus turns to "what I can do to make my marriage work," healing can begin.

Things to do or say:
1. Provide the opportunity for the controlled release of emotions, but disallow hurtful or spiteful attacks.
2. Let both parties know you are neutral. At some time talk separately with each person to get his or her unedited version.
3. Provide understanding of the issues involved. Point out options other than the drastic ones the couple may be considering, and help the couple work through those options.

4. Encourage the couple to talk *with* each other rather than *at* or *about* each other. Have them voice the things they would appreciate instead of saying what they don't like.

5. Remind them of the covenant they made with God on their wedding day and help them rebuild their marriage around self-giving *agape* love rather than self-seeking feelings or expectations.

6. For those already divorced, help them rebuild their spiritual, emotional, and family lives with the loving care and Christian standards of the church supporting them.

Things not to do or say:
1. Resist the urge to designate villains and victims or to take sides. Although fault may not be equal, it takes two people to make a marriage crisis.

2. Do not assume the responsibility to patch up the marriage. Only the couple can rebuild their relationship.

3. Do not condemn. People with faltering or fallen marriages know their failures and are loaded with guilt.

4. Do not underestimate the potential for violence in a domestic quarrel. Use caution entering a marital fight in progress.

5. Be cautious of unhealthy attractions or dependencies that can form between you and a counselee.

For further study:
Crabb, Lawrence J., Jr. *The Marriage Builder: A Blueprint for Couples and Counselors.* Grand Rapids, Mich.: Zondervan Publishing House, 1982.

Smoke, Jim. *Living Beyond Divorce: The Possibility of Remarriage.* Eugene, Ore.: Harvest House, 1985.

Snyder, Chuck and Barb. *Incompatibility: Grounds for a Great Marriage.* Phoenix: Questar Publications, Inc., 1988.

Wright, H. Norman. *Communication: Key to Your Marriage.* Ventura, Cal.: Regal Books, 1979.

Wright, H. Norman. *Marital Counseling: A Biblical, Behavioral, Cognitive Approach.* San Francisco: Harper & Row, 1983.

FOUR

SEXUAL MISCONDUCT

Lust is the ape that gibbers in our loins. Tame him as we will by day, he rages all the wilder in our dreams by night. Just when we think we're safe from him, he raises up his ugly head and smirks, and there's no river in the world flows cold and strong enough to strike him down. Almighty God, why dost thou deck men out with such a loathsome toy?

FREDERICK BUECHNER

In an age when some people wear the scarlet *A* more with the pride of conquest than the shame of disgrace, sexual sin still occasions crisis. Although practiced for centuries, adultery retains its ability to spark emergencies.

Premarital sex — *fornication*, to use a biblical term — casts an even wider shadow. Rare is the couple that enters marriage without prior intercourse, and an unintentional pregnancy or a broken relationship throws crisis into the picture.

Bogus sex bought through pornography or prostitution, violent sex acted out in rape, and twisted sex perversely found in sadomasochism or fetishes — to be out of control in any of these ways damages both the user and the used.

This chapter looks at the several crises caused by sexual misconduct.

A Misused Gift

In the fall 1982 issue of LEADERSHIP Journal, an anonymous pastor recounted his addiction to pornography. His crisis began one night on a trip, when he took a cab across town to see a former Miss Peach Bowl perform her exotic strip in a seedy bar. She was good at it, and he found it enticing. He began to search out movies, magazines, live acts — the gamut. He barely stopped short of hiring the body of one of the professionals.

Often he tried to stop. Such a "hobby" hardly squared with his Christian vocation. He felt dirty, lewd, sinful. It threw up a wall between him and God. It dominated his thoughts, even while preaching. He shuddered when he considered what his wife would think should she find out. Yet his will power toppled. Something that at first felt naughty and exciting became a brutal master, and even the enjoyment fled as he wanted more and more. He could cite the Bible passages that told him lust was wrong, only he couldn't stop.

Eventually after an emotionally flat moment in a live-act joint, followed by a weekend retreat in which he was the speaker but was speaking more to himself, he poured out his darkest secrets to a fellow pastor — a cherished and highly respected friend. "He listened quietly, with compassion and great sensitivity, as I recounted a few incidents, skipping over those that showed me in the worst light, and described some of my fears to him. He sat for a long time with sad eyes after I had finished speaking. We both watched our freshly refilled cups of coffee steam, then stop steaming, then grow cold. I waited for his words of advice or comfort or healing or something. I needed a priest at that moment, someone to say, 'Your sins are forgiven.'

"But my friend was no priest. He did something I never expected. His lip quivered at first, the skin on his face began twitching, and finally he started sobbing — great, huge, wretched sobs such as I had seen only at funerals.

"In a few moments, when he had recovered some semblance of self-control, I learned the truth. My friend was not sobbing for me; he was sobbing for himself. He began to tell me of his own expedition into lust. He had been where I was — five years before. Since that time, he had taken lust to its logical consequences. I will not dwell on the sordid details, but my friend had tried it all: bondage, prostitution, bisexualism, orgies."

The specter of where he might end up shocked the writer, and he began a search for answers. In the writings of François Mauriac, he found a greater reason for purity than merely not being bad. "Sins," Mauriac wrote, "are not a list of petty irritations drawn up for the sake of a jealous God. They are, rather, a description of the impediments to spiritual growth. We are the ones who suffer if we sin, by forfeiting the development of character and Christlikeness that would have resulted if we had not sinned." God, the pastor reasoned, had something more, better, to offer.

"The combination of grave fear struck in me by my pastor friend's grievous story and the glimmer of hope that a quest for purity could somehow transform the hunger I had lived with unabated for a decade prepared me to try once again to approach God in confession and in faith. . . . I cannot tell you why a prayer that has been prayed for ten years is answered on the 1,000th request when God has met the first 999 with silence. . . . [But] I prayed, hiding nothing (hide from God?), and he heard me."

There was still the matter of repentance. He told his wife and suffered with her through that aftermath. He took steps to avoid trouble spots. But the war within had subsided.

In that transformation, he found two rewards: a stunning new relationship with God that far exceeded his expectations, and a renewal of passion for his wife: "*Her* body, no one else's, is gradually gaining the gravitational pull that used to be scattered in the universe of sexes."

Divorced from love and giving and personalities and God's regulations, sexuality becomes an ugly, slavering master. Other obsessions bear resemblances to pornographic addiction. They, too, are displacements of the sexual energy meant to fire the love between husband and wife. Fetishes involve unusual objects of arousal. Sadomasochistic practices come from deep-seated feelings of worthlessness, guilt, and anger. Rape often has more to do with rage and inadequacy than with libido.

What to Do

People caught in the crisis of sick sex need intensive care. Their hurt and wounds have produced a perversion of one of their most basic drives. Condemnation hardly helps; they probably already hate themselves. They need comprehensive care, probably from specialists. And they need the spiritual wisdom and support of their pastor.

Crisis counseling involves several steps:

First, *help the person bring to the light what has been hidden.* Then the problem takes on specific dimensions and can be attacked. Denial plays a great part in continuing sexual problems; admission begins the healing process.

Because of this, the counselee needs a noncondemning listener who will help measure the dimensions of the problem. Many counselors ask questions such as: When did this start? How often do you do it? Have you ever quit for any significant length of time? What factors surrounded your return? When are you most tempted? How much of your time is taken in thought about this problem? Simply talking rationally and openly about the obsession begins the process of disarming it.

Second, *tackle the immediate legal, marital, or other social consequences.* A betrayed and disgusted spouse may need to be brought into the counseling. The problems of arrest or public disclosure or church discipline may need to be worked through. Counselees need a guide as they walk through these disheartening consequences.

Third, *develop a preliminary plan to break the habit.* The problem probably runs deep, but certain activities can be restricted immediately: trips to the kinky bar, taking certain magazines, spending time with acquaintances who share the misconduct. Structures of accountability can be set up. If the counselee binds himself to report any untoward activities to someone else, he has one more reason not to give in.

A wife, for instance, who inherits some of the bitter results of her husband's lust, certainly must be involved in the recovery. It's amazing how the very process of explaining lusts to one's wife dries up the wells of that lust. The idea is to encourage the counselee to make plans and report them.

The key at this step is the cooperation and absolute desire *N B* by the counselee to make a change. One way to increase the desire is to concentrate on what is being *lost* through continuing in unchecked lust, rather than in what must be given up "to be good." What finally captured the heart of the LEADERSHIP writer was the shining possibility of a *greater* passion for God. Nothing can replace gritty determination by the victim; no one can force a reversal of thinking or completely supervise a change of habits. But warm, encouraging support and wise suggestions from a pastor increase the probability of change.

Finally, *work toward fundamental changes of attitude.* Through skilled counseling, the behavioral roots of obsession can be laid bare: childhood factors, dubious self-perception, misunderstandings, past failures. Then a healthy and reconstructed ego can move toward appropriate sexuality. Most often this kind of care is beyond the limitations of a parish pastor, and most refer such cases.

But questions of sin and guilt and wholeness are precisely in the province of pastoral care. Only the Father can forgive. Only Jesus' work can cleanse. Only the Holy Spirit can empower a conscience to live in the light.

David Seamands, professor of pastoral ministry at Asbury Theological Seminary in Wilmore, Kentucky, recalls the help he gave a man in Christian leadership. "He said, 'My wife talked me into calling,' " Seamands remembers. "Bob had a letter of resignation written out and was about to deliver it to his church board, but his wife urged him to call me first. He had decided to resign because he felt completely unworthy to continue as a pastor. It seems he had been found in an unsavory place by the police. Bob was hooked on pornography, and that brought it to light. The police weren't giving him any problem, but his conscience sure was. Out of guilt, Bob had called a meeting of his board to tender his resignation.

"Bob was an outstanding young leader, and I wanted him to avert any rash decision. I told him, 'Bob, you wanted my opinion, so I'll tell you. Don't you dare do a thing like that! You have no right to do this to your people. They need you.'

"Bob shot back, 'But I have to do it. It's the only way to atone for this guilt. I'm loaded with sin.'

"I asked him how many people knew, and he said not many. I told him, 'Then I suggest keeping your mouth shut. What you need to do is work out an accountability relationship with three or four of your elders. Get yourself into good counseling, and let them hold you accountable for getting to the bottom of this problem and licking it. Don't just run away defeated.'

"Bob took me up on my advice. His elders didn't want him to resign. They loved him and appreciated his good work among them. He got the help he needed, kicked his problem, and stayed at his church. The last I heard, he was doing great."

Seamands's advice, formed in that particular situation, touched each of the four steps above.

Infidelity

Infidelity — adultery — draws many marriages to the pastor's office.

Duncan and Jenny Stewart weren't churchgoers, although Jenny had been raised in a strict Christian home on a Nova Scotia farm. Duncan came from a nominally Christian background, but in the last decade or so, weddings or funerals were all that got him into churches. His weekends were taken up with stock car racing. Still, when Jenny saw Pastor Bill Hamill's name in the paper concerning a Rotary speech, she asked her friend the bank manager about him. "What's he like? He's in Rotary with you, isn't he?"

"Oh, he's all right," the banker assured her. "He's a regular guy."

That's all Jenny needed to hear. She called him that afternoon at the church. "Reverend Hamill, do you ever talk with people about marriage problems?"

"Well, yes, I do," he replied, "but I don't really consider myself a marriage counselor. Are you having some difficulties in your marriage?" Jenny told him she was and scheduled an appointment for the following afternoon.

Things weren't good with Duncan. He knew more about water softeners than any two other technicians, but he had trouble holding down a job. While unemployed, Duncan was irritable and depressed, and Jenny was discouraged at his seeming inability to stick with a job. Jenny, a utility company assistant area manager, was obviously outdistancing him in career advancement.

Jenny and Duncan had learned to live with some of these tensions, but Jenny brought fears of another kind to Bill. "I think Duncan may be seeing another woman, and if he is, I'm not sure I can handle it."

"What makes you think that?"

"Duncan has always spent a lot of time working on stock cars, you know, as a mechanic, a pit crew member. He's always at a friend's garage with his head under the hood of some car. I mean, I wouldn't recognize him at night without a smear of grease on his face! But he'd always come home around 9:30, and we'd have a little time together before bed.

"Lately, however, he hasn't been getting home until nearly midnight, and I know the other guys aren't knocking off that late. He's also looking pretty clean and spiffy when he slips home. I'm not stupid. I think something's up."

"Have you talked with Duncan about it?" Bill asked.

"Oh, yeah. He gives me a story about dropping by the yard to check on his truck or going to see an old buddy and watching TV. I'm having a hard time buying it. He swears he's not messing around on me, but I don't trust the look in his eye."

Bill asked how she would feel if Duncan were indeed having an affair. She said she'd be shook; that's why she had come. Bill allowed her to voice her fears and told her he was glad she had come to see him. He made an appointment for a week later and encouraged her to bring Duncan. After Bill prayed for her and Duncan, Jenny left, feeling a little better.

When she arrived the following week, Jenny looked anything but relieved. "We had a big blowup last night. Duncan says he's moving out. He says he wants some breathing space or something. I don't want him to go, but he seems determined. I called him at work today, and he was planning to find an apartment this afternoon. For all I know, he'll be gone when I get back. Now what do I do?"

Bill was disappointed. He had hoped to get the two of them together to start them working on their problems. "I'm not sure what you should do," he honestly replied. "Has Duncan ever done anything like this before?"

"No, and that's what bothers me. Something is really different about him. He's distant. He seems preoccupied. He hasn't even been that interested in being close recently." At that Jenny needed a Kleenex. The competent executive was sobbing like a little girl. Bill spent the rest of the hour comforting Jenny and helping her sort her options. They set an appointment for two days later.

Jenny had her composure when she arrived, but she had a weary vacantness about her. "He's got a place to live over by the college in one of those apartments swarming with unmarried people. What's he up to?"

"I don't know, Jenny, but I wish we three could get together."

"Oh, that's right — he said to tell you he could take care of his own matters. I don't think there's a ghost of a chance I'll get him into this office now."

Without a couple to work with, Bill set out to help Jenny understand and handle what was happening in her life and to rebuild her Christian faith.

About five weeks later, Jenny brought some news to her weekly counseling session: "I got a call from Duncan's friend,

Mark, last night. He told me he didn't want me to be the last one to know: Duncan is seeing some woman on his soft-water route!"

"Is Mark sure? How does he know?"

"Oh, he's sure. I guess Duncan talks about her whenever they get together to work on the car. And besides, I talked with Duncan, and he couldn't deny it. As recently as last Tuesday, he was swearing there wasn't anybody else. That jerk lied to me! As if I didn't have enough problems. You know, right now I wouldn't take him back if he came crawling on his knees. That little floozy can have him!"

Before long, Duncan lost his job again, and evidently his affair turned sour. Jenny reported that he showed up on her doorstep with his handsome grin and a bottle of Chablis, begging her to take him back. "I was torn," she confessed, "but then I told him to take his wine and drink it in his own tacky apartment. I closed the door and ran into the bedroom and cried into my pillow until he quit knocking and shouting. That was last night. Did I do the right thing, Pastor? I don't feel good about it."

"Well, you and I have agreed that restoring your marriage is the number-one priority," Bill began, "but it can't be done on cheap terms. How do you think Duncan feels now?"

"He was pathetic last night. I'm sure he thought I'd be delighted to have him back. He was shook by the time he left. But you know, it's not all that satisfying to have him hurt. I think he's probably feeling pretty low."

"Then what do you think you ought to do?"

"I ought to take him back, be the good wife. But he hurt me! Can he just waltz back in and pretend nothing happened? Doesn't he *owe* me something?"

Bill let the question settle for a moment. "If you're talking about an apology — a genuine, from-the-heart apology — then, yes, he certainly does. If you mean you want to extract your pound of flesh, then I'm not so sure. Remember your marriage vow? Didn't you promise to love and cherish one another?"

"Yes."

"I thought so. That *love* you promised is supposed to be an enduring, God-type of love — *agape* love. *Agape* love just keeps on giving — even when the giving takes everything you've got. Duncan can't just "waltz back into your life" as if he'd gone out for a loaf of bread, but you've got to give him a chance to atone for his dreadful mistakes, his sin against God and you. Love gives another chance." He let his sermon sink in for a moment. "Jenny, do you think you've got that kind of God-given love in you? This isn't going to be easy."

Jenny sat quietly for a couple of minutes, although it seemed like twenty. A slow, contemplative "I think so" finally poured out of her heart. She wanted to give it another try.

"Jenny, I think you've made a decision that's best for both of you, and I honor you for your courage. Now, let's see if we can get Duncan here to put things back together. I think we can do it." With that, Bill jumped up and gave her a quick hug. That was a first, but he wasn't sorry he'd broken his own counseling rules. Jenny left the office that day steeled for what she had to do next: allow Duncan a second chance.

He moved home the next evening. Well, he brought back his shaving kit, his clothes, a few assorted dishes and utensils, and a gallon of souring milk. That was the extent of his apartment furnishings. But more than that, he brought back a broken and contrite spirit. He'd lost his job, his fling, and, with that, his self-respect. His wife, he realized, he didn't want to lose.

The next appointment brought together three people. Jenny had rejection, bitterness, and distrust to work through. Duncan had to come to grips with guilt, self-control, self-image, and accountability. He was pleased with himself for "making the right choice and being committed to the marriage." Jenny, on the other hand, needed reassurance of his honesty and commitment. "I'm not so ready to applaud your 'wonderful gesture'," she told him in one session. "You're only doing what you should have been doing all along. What about those nights when you were flitting about with *her*, and

I was home where I belonged, humiliated and hurting?"

In time, Jenny let go of her wounded pride. Duncan demonstrated his new fidelity by volunteering to always let her know where he was. Little tendernesses crept into their relationship. Shared words and kindnesses nourished the love they once had, and within a short time, they no longer came to Bill. Seven years later they're making a go of their marriage.

Counseling Commentary

That was a case that worked. Why? Let's look at the factors.

First, the marriage had something going for it before the shake-up. Duncan and Jenny did have a basic love and sense of commitment.

Second, Jenny hung on — despite being betrayed and humiliated. Going to Bill was a wise decision. He wasn't encouraging her to "look out for number one," or to "sue the cad's socks off." Instead, he wanted Jenny to have the personal substance to be able to give love and receive apologies should the time come. Had Jenny slammed and double-bolted the door behind Duncan, there would be no marriage today.

Third, Duncan passed his "silly season" and rededicated himself to the marriage. Surely probing what caused him to stray would be part of follow-up counseling, but for the time of crisis, his decision was what counted — an honest decision, not a cheap whitewashing.

But just when Duncan believed the worst trauma was behind them (he *had* come back, after all), for Jenny another trauma was beginning. Offenders often have a hard time understanding why the big deal when they return. But their spouses have had trust and self-assurance drained away and find it hard to open warm arms of acceptance.

The trick at this stage is to interpret to both sides those feelings at cross-purposes. Bill often found himself saying, "No, Duncan, the problem isn't quite over" and "Yes, Jenny, you need to reach deep to forgive."

Fourth, the full truth came out. It turned out this painful fling was Duncan's only infidelity. But had he had others, he would have had to tell Jenny.

Says Charles Shepson, "Further disclosures are extremely painful and temporarily make things worse. A new flood of hurt, anger, renewed betrayal, hopelessness, and distrust may sweep over the deeply wounded spouse. The offender feels that further disclosures may completely destroy all possibility of rebuilding trust. But the truth of the matter is that somehow full honesty is perceived, and so is dishonesty. Also, unconfessed affairs arising later prove terribly destructive and difficult to deal with. But after the initial renewed unpleasantness, true healing most often begins. With God's help it will take place."

In cases where the spouse doesn't know about the infidelity, David Seamands doesn't always advise breaking the news. "I've got to answer the question, Why tell the spouse?" he says. "Some burdens are best carried only with God. Do you tell a spouse only because you can't bear the burden yourself? What if it causes greater hurt? What if she can't bear it? If the story must be told, we pray together for the right timing and words. It's a terrible revelation to give anybody."

Fifth, the "other woman" stepped out of the picture. Duncan made a clean break with her after she dumped him, so she wasn't there to distract and destroy. Had she remained in the picture, Shepson would recommend instructing Duncan not to receive her phone calls and to forward any letters unopened.

Shepson asks for the right to read and answer such letters. In a pastoral way, he tells the woman that any further contact is not in their best interests. He writes, "His act of sending the letter to me demonstrates clearly his firm resolve before the Lord he loves to follow through on his commitment to his wife, his family, and his Lord. I'm sure you can respect him for that. It doesn't represent a rejection of you as a person, but rather a rejection of any further relationship with you." Without such a firm separation, further restoration is practically impossible.

At times when the mistress retains an unmistakable attraction to a wayward husband, David Seamands employs the power of the Lord's Supper. "When a guy tells me honestly, 'I'm hooked,' I ask him to join me for an hour-long time together. I tell him we won't counsel long — say, ten minutes. We'll spend the rest of the time in Communion together. After we talk about the problem for a while, we pray together and then take Communion. I give the sacrament time. We begin to think about Christ's body and our bodies and what we're doing with our bodies. I've seen the Lord's presence slowly but surely break the hold adultery has on the man. I'll do this almost every day for several days.

"I also assign great hymns to read and memorize. Deep emotional healing has to take place, and Communion and music touch us deeply. In sexual sin, ideas and feelings are in a shoot-out. Through the mystery of God's work through music and the sacrament, we do away with both thinking and feeling, and touch spiritual reality. I've seen God work in this way."

Sixth, Duncan and Jenny exercised patience. Rebuilding trust and even romantic love cannot be forced. Painful flashbacks are normal. Renewed sessions of hurt and distrust and wavering hope are common. By electing to report his whereabouts to Jenny, Duncan was giving her reason to trust him again. And she didn't have to demand it, which gave her reason to love him again. Jenny and Duncan met with Bill until they felt they were out of the water, and after that they continued working together to build their relationship. They understood what Shepson says: "Only weeds grow without attention."

One Thursday Duncan and Jenny invited Bill and his wife to join them in their hot tub Saturday evening. When the Hamills arrived, no one answered the front door. The Hamills rang again. No answer. So they pushed the door open and called to Duncan and Jenny. Still no answer. Figuring they must be in the hot tub already, the Hamills walked through the house to the patio. The lights were low around the pool, but the Hamills could make out two figures remarkably close together in the hot tub. Giving a cautious "Hi! We're here," the Hamills edged toward the patio.

Two panicked faces sank deeper into the hot tub and peered back. Duncan spoke immediately: "Whoa! Pastor Hamill! You startled us. Hey, uh, why — why don't you use the spare bathroom to get into your swimsuits."

Out of the corner of his eye, as he and his wife retreated into the house, Bill could swear he saw two arms hastily grab swimsuits. He chuckled all the way to the changing room.

Quickscan
SEXUAL MISCONDUCT

Immediate concerns:
1. The emotional stability of victims and victimizers demands first attention. Deep pain, anger, or hurt are in play.
2. You may need to try to forestall permanent "solutions" (quick divorce, violence, rash acts) born in anger or despair.

Keep in mind:
1. Lies foster marriage dissolution. Truthfulness may hurt like an incision, but it begins the healing process.
2. Lust has its attraction. It needs to be replaced with something better rather than preached into submission. The shining possibilities of truly knowing God or deeply experiencing marital love offer hope.
3. Sexual deviations usually require more than volition to be healed. Much has brought the person to this place; much needs to be done to move him or her into proper relationships. Prayer, spiritual healing, and competent counseling will probably have to team up to effect a change.

Things to do or say:
1. Hear the story. Let it all come out. It's probably been bottled up a long time.
2. Stand for righteousness, but in an inviting way that makes the right more compelling than the wrong.
3. In cases of infidelity, work with the couple if possible. If not, build up the will and emotional strength of the cooperative one to make that person prepared for the hard work of reconciliation, should it be possible.
4. Insist on the whole story being told to a spouse who knows any part of the infidelity. Buried secrets have a way of returning and destroying tentative new trust.
5. Use the power of prayer, Scripture, the sacraments, and great music to reach deeper than the intellect.
6. Radiate hope for the ability to make things right. Believe in the people even when they no longer believe in themselves.

Things not to do or say:
1. Do not denounce persons, only sin.
2. Do not neglect the seemingly strong party. Outward calm often masks seething internal emotions.
3. Do not allow confidences to be broken.
4. Do not expect easy resolution. Sexuality is a slippery creature difficult to capture and tame.

For further study:
Carnes, Patrick. *Out of the Shadows: Understanding Sexual Addiction.* Irvine, Cal.: CompCare Publications, 1985.
Mylander, Charles. *Running the Red Lights: Putting the Brakes on Sexual Temptation.* Ventura, Cal.: Regal Books, 1986.
Petersen, J. Allan. *The Myth of Greener Grass.* Wheaton, Ill.: Tyndale House, 1983.
Wilson, Earl D. *Sexual Sanity.* Downers Grove, Ill.: InterVarsity Press, 1984.

FIVE

DOMESTIC VIOLENCE AND ABUSE

On horror's head horrors accumulate.

WILLIAM SHAKESPEARE

All is not quiet on the domestic front. Homes sometimes erupt in anger and abuse. And the weakest are victimized the most.

Domestic violence and abuse can be physical, as in wife or child beating. Even battered husbands and abused elderly parents aren't uncommon. Sometimes it's sexual. It may even be emotional; there the cruelty is verbal, and words *can* hurt. In whatever form, domestic violence and abuse plunge the entire household into crisis. How can a pastor respond to these seemingly more prevalent and intensely difficult situations?

Child Abuse: Physical

Charles Shepson tells this story from his days in parish ministry: "One day I received an anonymous phone call. The woman said, 'There's a child being abused in a house two doors from your church. You need to help that poor little girl.' I couldn't get any more information before she hung up."

Shepson wondered, *How can I verify the information? What if the woman is mistaken or malicious? What if I blow the whistle on the wrong household?* So he hit on a plan. That day he began a neighborhood visitation program.

He didn't go to the suspected home first — a house itself showing neglect — but rather visited another. Then, when he called on the home two doors from the church, he could say honestly, "I'm from the church, and I'm visiting homes on the block. May I come in?" They invited him in.

It didn't take long, once inside, to confirm his suspicions. "The couple's little girl came into the room while we were talking," Shepson remembers, "and I tried to observe her unobtrusively. She looked about 3 years old, but she had no hair. Her legs and arms were thin and bony, and bruises were on her body. She had a dull, emaciated look. I was surprised to see her still in diapers at her age.

"I went to a judge and explained what I had seen. He called in the couple to question them. As it turned out, one was too drunk to show up, and the other arrived inebriated. It didn't take that judge long to concur with my findings. The judge removed the girl from the family and placed her with a Christian couple from our church.

"When they took the little girl home the first evening, the foster mom prepared to give her a bath. As she helped the little girl remove her clothes, suddenly the girl threw her arms over her head, shrank into a defensive posture, and whimpered, 'Don't hit me!' The woman wrapped her in her arms and assured her they would take good care of her."

Once the girl was in a loving family, she quickly had no need for the diapers. With a good diet, her hair started growing, and her frame filled out. She finally basked in the love and care every child needs.

Shepson entered this abuse crisis as many pastors do: not at the call of the principal parties. Child abuse often lodges in a family as a kind of cancerous disease. Many times it is passed from generation to generation; the abused become abusers. As a dark family secret, it's not about to be divulged. Spouses may ignore or rationalize their partner's behavior, partly out of a need to maintain a charade of family decency and partly from fear of the drastic consequences when the behavior comes to light. And the children often collaborate unexpectedly; family ties bind them in powerful ways. That means it's often an outsider who sounds the alarm.

With nothing more than an anonymous tip, Shepson didn't feel confident enough to bring in the authorities. Even the suspicion of child abuse can cast a dark shadow across a family's reputation. Child-welfare investigators want to be fair and discreet, but they are compelled to make a thorough investigation. It's not the kind of thing Shepson would wish on an innocent party. That's why he sought a diplomatic way to confirm the information.

Randy Christian, pastor to children and families at Beaverton (Oregon) Christian Church, wouldn't try to investigate. He advises, "In this case the evidence was easily seen. It isn't usually so, and ministers can actually impede official investigations by attempting their own, more subtle, investigations. I realize this is a judgment call, but I'd caution against private investigations." Pastors sometimes have to make tough calls, and this looks like one of them.

Once Shepson understood the situation, he wisely went to the authorities. Most counties have child protective services, child welfare agencies, or family services that are prepared to investigate accusations. The police or sheriff's department also can be notified.

This step involves heavy consequences: possible arrest, and with that removal from the family, possible loss of income, and community scorn. Criminal charges may be filed. Persons may go to prison. Homes may be broken apart. The list goes on, yet reporting such a crime remains necessary, and usually legally mandatory, if not easy.

Randy Christian suggests, "Given our Lord's advocacy for the child, the widow, and the defenseless, our first concern should be for the safety of the one unable to protect himself or herself. If an error is to be made, it will be in favor of safety for the defenseless."

Pastors, with good intentions, often want to keep matters within a small circle and try to take care of things quietly. Concern for the economic future of the family, the reputation of the church, and the legal fallout from abuse charges may push a pastor to resist calling the legal authorities. But simply chiding an offender to "go and sin no more" fails to underscore the depth of the problem. The abuser usually returns to his family and resumes the abusive behavior, the only response he may know.

Further, in most states pastors would have to break the law to *not* report a suspected case of child abuse. Reporting laws require pastors to do what Shepson did and what most professionals strongly recommend — blow the whistle.

Shepson followed up on the little girl and her family. She was placed in a Christian home, and for the first time received what she needed physically and emotionally — even spiritually. The parents, however, lost their daughter, incurred the wrath of the law, and continued on a path of drink and ruin. Shepson could not help them.

In many cases the parents are themselves victims — of their upbringing, of mental problems, of a series of bad choices, of unresolved anger and self-hate. We find it hard to sympathize with anyone who would hurt a defenseless child, yet these parents more often are sick, pathetic people than cruel, despicable maniacs. The arms of the church need to wrap around these victimized victimizers. In such ways as prayer, financial assistance for counseling, and providing supervised alternatives to incarceration, churches demonstrate their concern.

Child Abuse: Sexual

According to Michael Phillips, pastor of Lake Windermere Alliance Church in Invermere, British Columbia, and director of the local Communities Against Sexual Abuse group, "It is estimated that one out of four girls will be abused in some way before the age of 18. The figure is exactly half with boys, and the statistics are almost identical for the U.S. and for Canada." In over 90 percent of the cases, it isn't some seedy-looking character dragging a child into the bushes; it's Uncle Bob or Dad or the baby sitter or Mom's new boyfriend — or even Mom.

This kind of abuse throws a child's life into crisis. Writes Norman Wright in *Crisis Counseling*, "Abused children feel anger and rage, but at home they cannot express those feelings. They learn both to deny and to repress fear, anger, bitterness, and hatred. Any expression of their feelings leads to further repercussions that they want at all costs to avoid." So they learn to cope in other ways.

It's not unusual for abused children to slip into a make-believe world in which the bad things are happening to a made-up character, not themselves. They dissociate their bodies from the things happening to them. Michael Phillips identifies this as the Snow White syndrome: "Just as Snow White was poisoned and slept until Prince Charming came along, so the victim of sexual abuse often 'sleeps' through the abuse, hoping it will go away. One young girl even convinced herself that it was a girl she disliked who was the victim. She would accompany her father on excursions where she knew abuse was likely, hoping it wouldn't happen. When it did, she would transfer the abuse to her enemy while exiting into her own private world. For years she maintained that her father was a good man."

A Baptist pastor tells of a 13-year-old girl from his church who was plagued with recurrent epileptic seizures. For a young teen, she hardly talked, and she walked around with head down, blocking out most of the world around her. Her seizures had the doctors stumped. Finally her pastor, on a hunch, asked her, "Is there anything your mom or dad are doing to you that they shouldn't be doing?" That brought life into her. She vehemently insisted nothing of that sort had ever happened.

Her pastor read the signs but felt handcuffed since she was unwilling or unable to say anything. He spent the next three days praying for her, and her seizures actually got worse.

Her father came home drunk late the next night. He went straight to his daughter's room, got her out of bed, and took her into his room, closing and locking the door behind him. His wife was afraid of him when he got drunk, so she sobbed quietly in another room. The next morning the mother asked her daughter what had gone on. The girl finally broke down and told her mother of the sexual abuse, which had occurred for some time.

Mother and daughter went straight to their pastor. As the story unfolded, he felt a mixture of disgust and relief: disgust over the sordid details, and relief that they could finally stop the abuse. After talking briefly with them about what they had to do next, he accompanied them to the police station. The police arrested the father at work that very day. He would never again molest his daughter.

It would be nice if the story ended there, but the girl continued to have such trouble with her trauma-induced seizures that she finally had to be institutionalized. Her seizures worsened until she died at 19.

The pastor in the story found himself in a difficult bind. He strongly suspected that the girl was being molested, but he had neither proof nor the cooperation of the girl. Norm Wright says, "If you have a greater investment in helping a child than the child has in being helped, the results will be negligible." The pastor could pray and look for a way to draw out the girl, but the crisis was theirs, not his, and with nothing more than a hunch, he sadly waited for an entrée.

When the crisis finally arrived at his doorstep, the pastor faced two immediate concerns: the welfare of the girl and the curtailment of the father. The girl and her mother needed to be heard, comforted, and stabilized emotionally.

They also needed to be coaxed gently to report the offending father — something they knew would be costly. The wife would likely lose her spouse, her financial support, her home. The daughter would part with her only security and her privacy about a matter that was severely embarrassing. And so the pastor helped them walk through the procedure, supporting them all the way.

In other cases, sexually abused children call out for help. Michael Phillips tells of a girl who had been abused for three years by her policeman father. The father had told the family repeatedly of misused children whose complaints hadn't been followed up on, so she knew quite well that most abuse victims aren't believed. But after three years of intimidation, she told a social worker, who believed her. When the next official to enter the room, however, was a uniformed police officer, she began to weep uncontrollably. The moment was nearly lost.

The girl was more fortunate than many. "I discovered that victims of sexual abuse will disclose their painful story to an average of nine people before anyone believes them," Phillips explains. Because of this shocking statistic, *the first considera-tion for helping victims is to believe them*.

Anybody who has seen *The Crucible* about the Salem witch trials will naturally worry about children making up stories. Might they want to spite a parent or lie to get out of some kind of trouble? Phillips replies: "In five years of helping abused children, I've never found one child who has lied about being sexually abused. More often than not, they would rather say nothing, because the pain of being so intimately used is like an open wound that will not heal. In fact, statistics tell us only one in a thousand disclosures will be false, and some of those come from frantic parents who misread a child's statement. Such false claims are easy to check; the story changes with every telling. And among preadolescent victims, false claims are virtually nonexistent."

Besides believing a victim, the helper needs to communicate that message to the child. "I tell the child I believe every word he or she has said," relates Phillips. "If for some reason I can't honestly say this, I state that I believe they have been terribly hurt and the hurt can be stopped. Then I take the responsibility for informing the nonoffending parent or parents about the details of the abuse."

A second idea is to refrain from negative comments about the offending person. It can turn the victim, surprisingly, against the helper. The child can be greatly attached to the offender if that person is a parent or close relative. Says Phillips, "Most often a love relationship still exists, and the hope is that the 'wicked witch' will turn out to be 'Prince Charming' after all."

Phillips suggests pastors emphasize the volitional character of forgiveness, rather than running down the offender. "Forgiveness can be (and often must be) a cold, calculated act of the will. I find even preschoolers can understand what it means to forgive. The advantage we Christian counselors have is being able to introduce Jesus Christ into the situation. Since victims desire a Prince Charming, a Savior appeals to them. They often are prepared to accept the salvation and help the heavenly Father offers."

A third phenomenon to consider is the pain-pleasure factor, especially with older victims. After working over two years with one young woman, Phillips found she kept mentioning how guilty she felt. "Her guilt lay in the feelings she'd experienced during sex," Phillips recalls. "Though her mind was completely repulsed, her body did experience a degree of pleasure. As she entered puberty, the pleasure level increased. Though she knew what her father was doing had to be despicably wrong, her body would occasionally respond. Long after her father went to jail, she felt latent feelings of remorse for the pleasure her body had felt."

Phillips carefully explained how our bodies are built to feel pleasure even when we don't want them to. He had to reinforce that concept many times, especially when she began to feel sexual urges toward classmates and realized those feelings were similar to what she had experienced with her father. Phillips outlined the biblical understanding of sex as more than self-gratification. He also stressed that no child should ever have to have sex with an adult, and that the adult bears full responsibility for the act. This eventually helped her quit blaming herself and begin to understand the proper expression of sexual love.

A fourth item to keep in mind is overdependency. The victim easily can become overly attached to the helper. Phillips suggests avoiding long-term promises and stressing the helping role without becoming a surrogate parent to compensate for the past: "Make sure the victim knows your role and that you cannot be expected to be on twenty-four–hour call. One young victim would phone me an average of three to four times a day. At least once a day she would ask me to come over and counsel her. She hinted at suicide, as if my refusal would set off a regrettable but inevitable chain of events. The best answer was to involve her in the lives of several women in the church and encourage her to join groups such as Bible studies and prayer circles."

Two cautions: First, the women he selected to help had to be advised of her situation. This necessitated getting the victim's permission to tell them. Second, Phillips finds it unwise to place older abuse victims in situations where they have direct responsibility for younger children. "Sexual abuse is a power trip," he warns, "and one way to regain lost control is to abuse someone else."

Finally, the family needs the care of the church. Especially when the abusing person was a family member — often the breadwinner — the family experiences deep crisis. Along with family therapy, in which the whole family can learn how interactions can be better handled, the care and support of a church is a lifesaver. Many in the community will consciously or unconsciously shun the victim's family. People don't like to talk about such things or may consider the family "soiled." The special understanding and outreach of the church evidences the love of God, which writes off no one.

Spouse Abuse

In one way, spouse abuse is like suicide: the offender can think of no other suitable act to adequately express the depth of anger and frustration. For most, it's a learned response: Dad did it to Mom. For most, it's not volitional; they wouldn't calmly choose it from a list of appropriate responses were they sober and in control. For all, it is an inadequate and damaging way to respond to a loved one.

A pastoral counselor in a southern town tells of a couple in their early forties. "I'd been helping them with their marital problems," he says. "They had told of previous arguments that had dissolved into name calling and even a little pushing and shoving, but nothing major.

"Then one appointment the wife walked in sporting a big black eye. She and her husband both looked rather sheepish. It didn't take long for the conversation to turn to the woman's shiner. Sure enough, in the midst of a heated argument, the man had hit her in the face."

Sometimes people come up with elaborate excuses for such injuries. One woman I know swore she had fallen onto a door-knob. A few months later it was a box that had tumbled onto her as she fell off a ladder while getting it down. Not long after that, I went with the police (as police chaplain) when they answered a domestic disturbance call at the same home. It was no accident.

This couple, however, didn't deny the cause of the black eye. The counselor continues: "The husband took responsibility for what he did. He was ashamed and couldn't begin to excuse it. It turned out he had a difficult time with anger. He didn't consider it a legitimate part of his emotional arsenal, and so he suppressed it most of the time. He had a negative self-image and felt tremendous guilt whenever that anger boiled to the surface, such as it did in the argument with his wife. With no legitimate way to recognize his anger and deal with it little by little, he was left with recurrent outbursts in which his anger exploded beyond control. I eventually referred him to a group of men who all were dealing with anger. The group therapy worked well.

"The wife, as with many victims of abuse, maintained some sense of deserving what she got. Without knowing it, she actually helped incite his outbursts and then gained a certain amount of satisfaction from being the wronged party. I helped her find a therapy group for women working on self-image.

"Of course, we talked about what the shiner meant to each person. We did a biopsy on the fight that led to the husband striking the wife. Before we were finished, they could see what caused the violence, and they had an idea of how to avoid it. I got them jointly to take responsibility for their parts in causing the problem. Then we dealt with the pain and shame both were feeling."

As both partners began to feel better about themselves, they were better able to avoid the name calling and shoving. Their pastor helped them learn how to be assertive rather than aggressive, to make pacts and keep them, and to fight fairly.

"Since violence is often picked up and acted out by children in a family where the parents fight," the counselor continued, "I included the kids in family counseling. They needed to see how families can resolve difficulties without abuse. Otherwise they'd become prime candidates for domestic troubles when they grow up."

In this instance, the husband appeared to be gaining control of his anger. Everyone agreed that it wouldn't be necessary for the wife to leave the home. "I told her," her counselor said, "that she has to make it clear to her husband that she *will* call the police if he ever strikes her again. And it can't be a bluff; she has to intend to follow through. Otherwise she becomes an enabler, co-dependent on violence to solve problems. Spouses who fail to report physical abuse simply reinforce bad behavior. And any first-year psychology student knows that reinforced behavior continues."

Long before counselors have the luxury of trying to bring harmony to a marriage, though, they have to concern themselves with basic safety: Will the spouse be in danger of further battering? If so, then immediate arrangements have to be made to separate the couple.

Many communities provide shelters for abused wives and children. Relatives will often take in a victim. Church members may be willing. I know our spare bedroom has provided shelter for a night or two. The important factor is that the threatened spouse find a place free from the possibility of bodily harm — and not feel sub-Christian for exercising that basic right.

Then the work of reconciliation and rebuilding is at hand. The pastor in our example handled this phase well. He had the advantage of knowing the couple, and he benefited from their candor. His first tactic was to get them to understand what went on prior to the violence that sparked it. This helped the couple see the several points in the argument where it probably could have taken a more productive turn. It also helped the couple discover their joint responsibility for both the mistake and its positive resolution.

He did more; he found ways to build up both the husband and the wife so they could approach their marriage from strength rather than dysfunction. Involving the rest of the family also helped and, we hope, prevented the continuation of abuse into another generation.

Sexual abuse of a spouse often has less to do with sex than with violence, power, rage, control. The rapist uses sex to act out violent and angry intentions against his victim. And to force one's spouse into any sexual act against his or her will is a form of rape.

Again, no man or woman, married or not, must give in to sexual demands contrary to conscience or will. Pastors can encourage the victim to seek safety first and then work toward resolution of the problem if the spouse is willing. The rest of the intervention needs to focus on the dynamics that make sexual aggression the chosen form of abuse, and those factors in the victim that have encouraged or allowed it.

Counselors need to be aware of their feelings in spousal abuse situations. The pastor who counseled the couple over the black-eye incident confessed, "When I first saw that blackened eye, I wanted to give the fellow a shiner, too! All my protective urges rush to the surface at a time like that, and I had to curb them to be able to deal effectively with the couple and not just get indignant for the woman."

Personal safety is not a foolish concern for interveners in abuse situations. According to a 1976 *Psychology Today* article, fully 25 percent of police fatalities and 40 percent of on-the-job injuries arise from intervening in domestic crises.

Fortunately physical violence isn't the rule, even among cases into which the police are called, but wise is the pastor who steps cautiously into potentially dangerous circumstances. Fear ought not preclude intervention, but neither should folly accompany it.

Quickscan
DOMESTIC VIOLENCE AND ABUSE

Immediate concerns:
1. Be aware of the potential for continued or more severe violence and abuse. The victim's safety — and your own — are of primary concern
2. A victim should not stay in a situation where violence or abuse threatens. Pleas of "It won't happen again!" are suspect.
3. Call the police for any violence or abuse in progress, and follow their instructions.
4. Do not promise strict confidentiality. You may not be able to keep the promise, either legally or morally.

Keep in mind:
1. Abused children won't necessarily expect you to believe them. They may not divulge information harmful to the abusing parent.
2. Small children nearly never make up sexual abuse charges. They cannot make up something about which they know nothing.
3. Spouse abuse is rarely a chosen response. It is a response born in passion and frustration. Self-hatred and poor coping mechanisms often underlie the problem.
4. Spousal sexual abuse is not something an unconsenting spouse must bear. A spouse should not be violated sexually merely because he or she is married to the violator.
5. The presence of genuine guilt doesn't necessarily indicate the end of a battering problem. Most batterers express remorse when anger subsides; many repeat their behavior.
6. Reporting abuse, as difficult as it is, must be done. Families will need support as they go to the authorities.

Things to do or say:
1. Secure the bodily safety of the victim.
2. Show love, concern, warmth. Remain unshocked by what happened. The victim needs to be able to relate the story without inhibition.
3. Listen for cryptic comments from children. Role playing, using anatomically correct dolls, and having them make crayon drawings are other ways to obtain information.
4. Remove the notion that "Christians never do such things." All victims need to be believed, even when the accused is a Christian.
5. Help the victim and victimizer find specialized care.
6. Use a tape recorder with the permission of the victim. Tapes may well convince a skeptical parent or other authorities.
7. Report child neglect and abuse to the proper authorities. It's required by law in most states.

Things not to do or say:
1. Do not assume an innocent parent was unaware of child abuse. Denial is common.
2. Do not castigate the abuser. You may lose the cooperation of the victim, who often loves the abuser anyway.
3. Do not ask a child "Why?" questions. They are not sophisticated enough for analysis of the problem. Stick to finding the facts.
4. Do not underplay the potential for continued or increased violence in domestic fights.
5. Do not reject offhand any report of abuse. Tend toward believing it first, and then seek to validate it.

For further study:
Martin, Grant L. *Counseling for Family Violence and Abuse.* Waco, Tex.: Word Books, 1987.
Olson, Esther L. and Kenneth Petersen. *No Place to Hide.* Carol Stream, Ill.: Tyndale House Publishers, Inc., 1982.
Strom, Kay Marshall. *Helping Women in Crisis.* Grand Rapids, Mich.: Zondervan Publishing House, 1986.

HOMOSEXUALITY

The true "orientation" of Christians is not what we are by constitution, but what we are by choice.

JOHN R. W. STOTT

Homosexuality — a word with greatly differing connotations. On the one hand are gay liberationists celebrating their emergence from the closet with odes to the tune of "Gay is okay!" On the far distant hand are "queer bashers" intent on harassing individuals they consider to be fair game for cruelty.

In between rests uneasily a spectrum of folks — Christian and agnostic, trendy and traditional — trying to make sense of the still-evolving understanding of the causes and realities of homosexuality. Some push more toward tolerance, others toward condemnation, but they want to do it with understanding rather than bumper-sticker philosophies.

But the fact remains: homosexuality causes crises. For the one who discovers personal affection for the same sex. For parents and other relatives who learn of it. For a society facing issues of public health and human rights. And for a church whose sons and daughters veer from the standards of the centuries.

The crisis we'll focus on here is the personal one: the crisis of those who confront their homosexuality as well as those affected by that discovery.

(A word about semantics: *Homosexual* describes only one

aspect of a person who may also be a truck driver, a parent, a hero, a Christian. When I use the word *homosexual*, therefore, it is shorthand for "a homosexual *person*," whose homosexuality is but one aspect of a diverse life. When I employ the word *gay*, I in no way endorse the gay lifestyle. Though *gay* was coined by homosexual persons to cast off negative implications of *homosexual*, I use it merely for convenience, for much of the lifestyle of gay people is anything but happy.)

Much can be said about homosexual orientation and behavior — Is it chosen or discovered? — but I'll leave that for others to debate. The assumption in this chapter is that homosexual *orientation* is not, in itself, a sin. It may be a given at birth, or it may be chosen somehow through complex psychosocial processes not completely known or understood, even by the gay person. But whatever the cause of the orientation, what one *does* with it is a choice. Therefore, in accord with the Scriptures, homosexual *behavior* is wrong, just as biblically proscribed heterosexual behavior is wrong.

The key distinction: While we denounce homosexual behavior as sinful, we do not deplore the homosexually inclined person holding the behavior in check. While we hate the sin, we cherish the person trying valiantly not to sin.

"Homosexuals can and do change and experience fulfilling heterosexual marriages," say some. And to back it up is powerful anecdotal evidence of former homosexuals happily married.

"No! Once a homosexual, always a homosexual," say others, "and besides, it would be a sin against one's God-given nature even to attempt to change one's sexual orientation." To the evidence of changed lives, they respond, "He never was a true homosexual. You can't change true homosexuals."

This chapter stands on the side of those who say change is possible. The evidence of lives transformed by the power of God is irrefutable. Some former homosexuals live like dry alcoholics — one day at a time — knowing they remain only a slip away from returning to their affliction. Others appear miraculously transformed within, so that even the temptation seems a vague memory. In either case, <u>change is possible</u>. To provide tools for pastors to use to help those in homosexual crises is the purpose of this chapter.

An Awful Awakening

Pastor Carl Wasser awoke with a start. It felt like the ringing phone had lodged somewhere in his spine. Carl half shuffled, half dashed to the kitchen. The clock glowing on the microwave told him it was 2:37. "Hello?"

"Oh, I'm so glad you're there!" The voice was male, and it sounded tense. Commotion filled the background. "I'm really sorry for getting you up like this, but I need your help. I'm in jail."

The circuits in Carl's mind had warmed up by now. "May I ask who this is?"

"Oh, I'm sorry. This is Ted Klein — you know, Art and Edna's boy." Of course Carl knew him. His parents were deeply involved in Meadowwood Community Church, and Teddy — that's what everyone called him — had grown up in the church. Now he was in college across town.

"You're in jail? What kind of trouble are you in?"

"Look, I need you to come bail me out." Ted avoided answering the question. "I can give you the money tomorrow, but I need to get out of this place tonight. I get only one call, so I called you. Can you help me? I know it's a lot to ask."

"Are your mom and dad out of town? Why didn't you call them?" Carl could dodge questions, too.

"Hey, I couldn't do that! No way. They'd just die. I turned to you because you're my minister and I need help. Can't you just come get me?"

"Ted, what are you in for? Why can't you tell your parents?"

"I'd rather not say over the phone. Look, won't you please come help me?"

Carl wasn't without a heart. "Okay, Ted. It'll take me about thirty minutes. How much is your bail?"

"Better bring a couple hundred bucks."

"I'm on my way. But one thing: when I get there, I'm going to expect some straight answers."

All the way downtown, Carl wondered if he were doing the right thing. *Should I have called Art? Why won't the kid say what the matter is? What kind of fool am I to be traipsing downtown at this hour of the night? What's Teddy up to, anyway? What can I do to help him?*

He pulled into the parking lot and found the jail entrance. From the open windows above, gruff voices and cursing filtered through the iron mesh. *I can see why he doesn't want to spend the night!* Carl thought as he blinked in the bright light of the doorway.

"I'm here to see Theodore Klein," Carl told the desk sergeant. "I believe he was arrested earlier this evening."

The sergeant straightened up and squinted at Carl. "You his father?" It wasn't a particularly nasty look, but it wasn't friendly, either.

"No, I'm not. I'm his pastor."

"Pastor!" Now he looked genuinely amused. "You know what we hooked him up for? We caught that little dirtbag parked by the city pool with two prostitutes — *male* prostitutes!" The sergeant paused to see what kind of response that would raise.

Carl's face blanched, but he retained his composure. "Can I bail him out?"

"Yeah. We'll be glad to get rid of him. That'll be two hundred bucks, and he'll have to promise to appear for a preliminary hearing in the morning." Carl handed over the money, collected one grateful and scared kid, and drove toward the college.

The car was filled with awkward silence. Finally Carl spoke. "The officer told me why you were arrested. You know you're going to have to tell your parents."

"I know," Ted replied, hanging his head. "Would you help me? I don't even know where to begin."

"You'll have to do the talking, but, yes, I'll stay with you while you do it. Just tell them the truth."

When they got to the college Ted reluctantly made the call.

His parents were stunned. After Ted told them the bare bones, Carl spoke reassuringly to them: "Ted's okay. He's got a hearing at 9 A.M. Yes, I'll attend with you." At 4:30 Carl finally crawled back into bed.

The next several days Carl spoke frequently with Ted and his parents. He walked them through the hearing the next day. Ted didn't get any jail time, but he was pretty shaken by the severity of the legal process. He realized he was in real trouble.

His parents were in shock. First they couldn't believe it was true, and then they had to struggle to keep from blowing up at Ted. In quieter moments they wondered how this could happen in their good Christian home. "We feel like we've failed Teddy somehow," Edna told Carl. "Are we to blame? I can hardly look my friends in the face." Art, a man of few words anyway, sat through counseling sessions in near silence.

In several conversations with Ted, Carl discovered the extent of Ted's homosexuality. Ted claimed to have noticed an attraction to other boys for a number of years. In high school he tried dating girls and wanted to think he didn't have a problem, but he didn't feel successful in his social experiments. By college, he had decided he was homosexual, although he hated himself for it. He knew it was wrong, but he seemed pulled irretrievably toward his urges.

That night with the two male prostitutes was only his third real episode of homosexual activity. It came on the heels of a couple of failed tests at college. He couldn't account for the vast departure from his normal habits, and he was mortified that he was caught, but he wouldn't exactly come to grips with his problem. "That's just the way I am," was his most frequent explanation. This worried Carl, but he couldn't extract something from Ted that Ted was unwilling to give.

Ted was lucky in one sense; news of his brush with the law didn't hit the papers. As far as Carl knew, only Ted and his parents were aware of Ted's problem. And none of them was about to let the church know.

Before long, Ted had moved his things out of his parents' home. He moved in with a single guy from the church. Jeremy, his housemate, was straight; he just needed someone to share the rent. Carl wondered, *Should I tell Jeremy about Ted? He ought to know, I suppose, but I can't break confidence with Ted*. Carl said nothing.

About two months later Jeremy came to Carl in private. "I'm getting reports of something pretty bad about Ted. He's been bringing some younger guys into his room, and it doesn't look very good to me. I suspect he's gay. What should I do?"

Now Carl was mad. *What does Ted think he's doing?* "Jeremy, can you help me by asking Ted to knock off the entertaining of guests? We don't want people getting suspicious about Ted." Carl was purposely vague with Jeremy. The tone of his voice said this was important, but Carl didn't want to alarm Jeremy or reveal Ted. Jeremy said he'd ask Ted to keep down the traffic.

When Carl got Ted into his office, he laid things on the line: "Ted, you listen to me, and you listen good. I know about the various guys you've had to your room. You've got Jeremy — and who knows who else — feeling pretty funny about you. How old were those young men? Were any under age? You're still on probation. Do you know what that means? They can put you away in jail for years! Do you hear me — years! This has got to stop, Ted. It's wrong. You need help. You need to confess. You can't keep on shaming yourself. You're hurting other people and grieving God! And you know what happens to people like you in jail . . ." Carl wanted to scare Ted. If an appeal to control and morality didn't stop him, maybe fear would.

Ted looked shook, sure enough, but through tears he blurted out, "You just don't understand. I can't help myself. Do you think I want to do this? Maybe this is just the way I am. Maybe I'm supposed to be different. How do you know you're so right? Are you perfect?" The tears had turned to a kind of rage.

"Ted, deep down, do you feel good about what you've done? Is this the way you want to be? Don't you want to change? Let God help you." It wasn't the first time Carl had offered this lifeline, but perhaps this was the most adamant offer.

Ted pulled into a hard little shell. "I don't have to listen to this. You don't have any control over me. I'm going to do whatever I want."

Carl started grasping at straws: "Well then for heaven's sake, if you won't control yourself, the least you can do is exercise some responsibility! Stay away from the younger ones. Can't you stick with your own age?"

Ted remained marginally tied to the church. One of his interests was drama, and he sometimes took part in skits as part of the Sunday evening services. One Tuesday Carl ran into a parishioner in Denny's. As they were walking out to the parking lot together, the man lowered his voice. "Carl, you know Kenny, the high school senior we're keeping as foster parents? Well — you can take this as you will — he told me at prayer time last night that the guy playing the golfer in the skit last Sunday, he, uh, that guy had propositioned him once at the Tastee Freez. When I asked Kenny if he was certain it was the same guy, he said he was sure. What do you know about Ted?"

Carl had to answer. "He's having some troubles right now. I'll talk with him and see if I can clear this thing up." From that point on, Ted wasn't allowed to represent the church in any leadership position, although he was encouraged to attend church.

Later, Ted began dating a girl from the church. Carl viewed this as a good sign, although with mixed emotions. After they had dated pretty steadily for a number of weeks, the young woman made an appointment with Carl. "Pastor," she said, sitting on a couch across from his chair, "you know Ted and I have been dating. I like Ted, and I'm not even sure this is a problem, but my friend encouraged me to talk to you. I'm not sure exactly how to say this, but Ted has . . . has difficulty expressing any affection. Is he gay?"

Carl swallowed hard. "Cindy, that's something *you're*

going to have to ask him. Think about it for a minute; if Ted were gay and I knew it, would I have the right to tell you?"

Cindy did ask Ted, and to his credit, he told her the truth. They struggled through a few more weeks of dating, but it was too big a hurdle to cross.

By this point many in Meadowwood Church were catching on. Most felt concern more than condemnation. They wanted to help but didn't know where to start. When one fellow collegian confronted Ted about his homosexuality, Ted told him, "It's really my business, not anyone else's. And besides, Pastor Wasser told me it's okay as long as I'm responsible about it." When that statement found its way to Carl's study via a shocked parent, Carl about hit the ceiling. Ted was using a statement born in frustration in a way Carl had never intended.

Carl asked Ted to come and see him. This time Ted's anger and bravado were gone. He obviously was wrestling with his sexual identity and the accompanying lifestyle. As the session ended, Ted rose and looked at Carl. "I wish you were my dad. Would it be all right if I give you a hug?"

Without blinking, Carl answered, "Sure, if you do it appropriately." Then he grabbed Ted in a fatherly bear hug.

Ted moved, not long after that, to San Francisco. Now and then Carl gets word from Art and Edna that he's "doing okay." That's their way of saying Ted hasn't given up a homosexual lifestyle.

Crisis counseling with homosexuals can be frustrating.

Compassion without Condolence

Carl's role with Ted was difficult from the start. Ted wanted a rescuer to shield him from undesirable consequences. Just as alcoholics may have people who contribute to their addictive behavior, so may homosexuals have people who unwittingly encourage them to continue. A man's behavior normally has to become a major crisis for him to realize he has to do something. If a pastor plays along with a rescue game, the scene will be replayed.

For a similar reason, Hal B. Schell, director of the Spring Forth ministry of the Teleios Counseling Center at College Hill Presbyterian Church in Cincinnati, rarely contacts homosexuals at the request of relatives. He strongly urges relatives to convince the person to contact him. An old joke asks: How many psychologists does it take to change a light bulb? The answer: Only one, but the light bulb has to really want to change. Many pastors, like Carl, find this to be true with homosexuals. The number one criterion for the success in *NB* crisis intervention is the desire of the homosexual person to change. Without that, all the good intentions and techniques by the counselor will have little effect. That desire to rebuild from ground up evidently was missing in Ted.

A second necessary component is the homosexual's positive expectation to be able to change. Ted's one refrain was that he was what he was. He'd wanted to change as a high school student. Presumably when he dated the girl, he'd wanted to change. But he hadn't changed, and so he believed he couldn't change.

Even those who would like to change will not if they remain convinced that such change won't happen. And the gay movement shouts loud and clear that it cannot.

Therefore, hope remains one of the greatest gifts a Christian counselor can offer a desperate homosexual. "When Jesus said he makes all things new," one pastor said, "I don't think he meant all things except the lives of those who are sexually disoriented. Certainly the transforming power of God can work in this area of life. If not, what does *omnipotent* mean?" Pastors may have to outlast the inner doubts of a discouraged and defeated homosexual. The message of hope is that those who want to change and who believe change is possible can change. God transforms lives.

Counseling Guidelines

Let's see how well Carl's technique stacks up against a set of guidelines used by Hal Schell. The ministry at College Hill Presbyterian is known nationwide as one in which people

have found life-changing recovery from problems of homosexuality. Hal and the others in this ministry have worked
with over six hundred men and several dozen women. Not all
have emerged victorious, but many have, and many others
are on their way. In their experience, they've found these
factors important:

● *Reasonable confidentiality.* The shame involved in homosexuality is nearly all-consuming. For strugglers to open up
even enough to give their names or addresses is a major step.
They have to feel certain their identities will not be divulged.
Many realize that to be found out can mean the end of a
marriage, the loss of employment, the ridicule of an uncaring
society, and the estrangement of family and friends. Keeping
the secret hurts them terribly, but letting it out is a danger they
fear they cannot allow.

As it did Carl, this situation can put pastors in a bind. Didn't
Jeremy have a right to know about Ted? After all, his reputation could be impugned. And how about the situation with
the young men Ted was seeing — shouldn't it be stopped? If
there were minors involved, technically wasn't Carl breaking
the law not to go to the police with his information? These are
questions every pastor must face.

When a parishioner told Carl what his foster boy had said
about Ted, Carl answered vaguely about Ted having some
"troubles." Then he saw to it that Ted's taking a visible leadership role be curtailed.

The young woman dating Ted asked Carl a straight question: "Is Ted gay?" Carl didn't want to lie, nor did he want to
break a confidence. He chose a wise course: neither denying
nor confirming her suspicions, but instead having the woman
ask Ted.

Retaining confidentiality can be tricky. Some pastors
choose to tell counselees from the outset: "I may not choose to
keep everything you tell me strictly confidential. I will by all
means be *responsible* with any information you give me, but I
cannot promise to keep everything an absolute secret. If you
appear to be a danger to yourself or others, I may need to
inform them or the appropriate authorities, as law compels

me. And I may want to involve other leaders of this body of Christ in the process of healing and restoration. I want you to understand my position from the beginning."

This may cut into counselee candor, but it does protect the counselor and give him or her options as the counseling proceeds. It's a choice counselors must make.

Confidentiality shouldn't apply to spouses, Schell contends. Where there is a spouse, he insists on involving that person. "It's completely unfair, and even dangerous, for a married partner to remain unaware of a spouse's homosexual infidelity," he explains. "It's possible now to kill a spouse with AIDS contracted in a homosexual affair. A spouse simply *has* to know. Secrets in a family can be more destructive than adultery. The homosexual needs to confess guilt and shame, and the couple must work on the resolution together."

● *No condemnation.* Homosexuals as a whole are among the most self-condemning individuals. And among homosexual persons from a Christian background, the self-condemnation is even greater. Part of the strength of the gay liberation movement is its simplistic answer for guilt: forget it. Many Christian homosexuals won't buy that. Yet they're left with no apparent relief. The last thing they need is heavy condemnation.

One plant worker made the mistake of propositioning the boss's son in the rest room. The indignant son took the matter to his father, who took the case to the church board, because the worker was a church member and the boss was a board member. The pastor and board confronted the young man, and he confessed. They had him confess before the whole church and display signs of repentance. They then forbade his attending the church for the next six months. A year later the man is still in counseling.

Somehow, grace was lacking in that episode. What other sin, following confession and repentance, would bar a church member from attending worship? Would adultery? Murder? If restoration and healing were desired, then the church worked against their best interests.

Homosexuals in crisis need people who will not reject them at first mention of homosexuality. They need unflappable, consistent guides who will care about them and hear them out while offering a better way.

Carl was firm about where he stood concerning homosexual practice. Ted knew with certainty that Carl opposed it, because all of Carl's counsel was predicated on that biblical stance. Ted also knew, however, that Carl cared about him as a person. Neither Carl nor, later, the church pushed Ted out of their fellowship and worship. They kept Ted among them, where they hoped to impact his life.

Ted did misuse this trust. He grossly twisted Carl's last-ditch advice to be at least responsible if he would not be moral. He wavered between accepting a Christian understanding of his homosexuality and falling back to a gay liberationist position. But even as he wavered and fell, he had people who cared about him, people who were not condemning him as a person although they wouldn't bend on the sinfulness of his behavior.

● _Accountability_. "Once I have gotten to know a counselee, I make a pact with him," Schell says. "I tell him, 'You're working to keep from acting out your homosexual urges. That's good, and I'll be praying for you that you don't fall into temptation. But if you do continue to act out your fantasies, I expect you to tell me when that happens. There can be no games between us, no secrets. I've got to know. That way, together we can determine what circumstances are working against you to make you fall, and together we can plot some strategies to break those patterns."

Gay people have a tough time being accountable even to themselves. Those who consider themselves in crisis probably don't like what they are doing, yet they haven't gained self-control. Having to tell someone about a homosexual episode may keep that episode from happening.

The counselor also needs to retain an accurate picture of the problem. A person plagued with only a homosexual fantasy life obviously needs different counseling from one who daily visits gay bath houses. The one who falls as an isolated incident after a long period of chastity needs different help from the one who repeatedly ends up in liaisons after swearing the previous one was the last. When counselees honestly report their activities, counselors have more to work from.

Ted wasn't very good about reporting to Carl and appeared unwilling to face the extent of his problem. Ted wanted momentary rescue rather than complete change, and until he becomes ready to acknowledge his problem and place himself in Carl's hands, Ted ties those hands.

● *Team counseling.* A crisis response may need to be solo, but the continuing efforts of a counselor are best made in tandem. "Don't counsel alone," warns Schell. "Suppose you meet privately a number of times, and then out of spite or frustration he accuses you of improper advances. How do you defend your reputation? For protection, for the person's accountability, and to take advantage of another's discernment and prayer, we counsel in pairs."

But what about pastors who don't have the luxury of trained associates? "Many churches have a disciplinary committee made up of spiritually mature elders or other church leaders. I'd probably sound out the one I felt was most able to be of help. I'd talk about such cases in general and see how the leader responds. If I felt the person could provide loving but firm help, I'd ask the counselee if we could involve that person in the process," Schell recommended. A fellow pastor or outside counselor are other possibilities.

Carl was caught at this point. When Ted spread the notion that Carl had approved of his "responsible" homosexual practice, Carl had to rely on his good name and theological track record to convince his church that he had said no such thing. He could have benefited from a companion in the counseling process — and so might have Ted.

The Crisis behind the Crisis

What brings homosexuals to pastors is often one of two things: a person finally concedes his or her preference for the same sex, or he bumps into some disturbing consequence of homosexual behavior, such as arrest, disease, or discovery. In either event, an ordered world has been disordered, and the person needs help reconstructing it.

Initially the pastor's role is presence. The homosexual in crisis needs someone. The genuine, unshockable, noncondemning presence of a caring Christian provides much-needed support.

The temptation is to treat the immediate crisis, but the ultimate cure comes in working on the causes of the homosexuality. Does the counselee know and understand the roots of his behavior? What specific activities has he done, and how often? How long-standing is the behavior?

Since many people experience passing episodes of same-sex attraction or sexual experimentation, especially when young, counselors are loathe to label a person a homosexual without enduring evidence. Some crisis counseling never goes beyond this point; the person is not a homosexual, after all.

But for those whose crisis is real, the counselor searches for triggering mechanisms. Hal Schell recalls meeting many times with a man we'll call Ron. He noticed Ron's lack of assertiveness and confidence. They talked about his sexual history.

Ron's greatest problem was pornography with a homosexual slant. He was addicted to it but knew it was wrong. Ron had previously experienced a limited number of homosexual liaisons, but wasn't regularly having sexual contact. During this time, Hal was gaining information about Ron and helping Ron understand himself and his reasons for his homosexual behavior.

That brought them to the action stage. There's a time to listen and a time to confront. How do you know the time for action? "When they start volunteering information, detailing their fantasies, allowing me insight into their family life — that's when I sense I've gained the right to be heard," Schell explains. "They trust me, and I've got some material to work with. As a counselee relates a recent experience, such as a visit to a gay bath house at a low moment, I can start to tie that with earlier behaviors and make associations: 'Do you realize that whenever you feel put down in any way, you react by seeking sexual encounters? Are you looking for sex or something else?'

"It's important that they see the connection, what triggers their behavior. One theory advanced by Leanne Payne, author of *The Broken Image* and *The Crisis in Masculinity*, suggests an analogy with cannibalism. Cannibals didn't eat people for nourishment. They chose people with characteristics they admired — strength or intelligence or bravery — and ate them, expecting to take on those characteristics. Payne believes such symbolic confusion is at work subconsciously in the homosexual male: he thinks he lacks masculinity, so he seeks ever more of the male organ to compensate. But he can't ever get enough. Lesbians seem to be searching more for emotional dependency, and a smaller segment of them are promiscuous."

After a long fourteen months, Ron suddenly "saw the light." Hal had given him the book *Homosexuality and Hope* by Gerard Van den Aardweg, and in reading it, Ron found himself. "This is my life!" he told Hal. Finally he was ready to throw off his old life and receive a new one. Ron still had to reorient his life. Hal helped him take the first few steps of obedience: destroy his pornographic magazines, change some patterns of life to keep away from temptation, consider the idea of dating women.

Before long, a former girlfriend entered the picture. Schell and his wife nurtured Ron through a courtship, and about six months later Ron announced his impending marriage. "Ron had become a totally new man," Schell says. "Where before he was trying — unsuccessfully — to use his own will to fight his homosexuality, now he was leaning on the Lord's will. He got married and is now actively involved helping others struggling with homosexual orientation. He's no longer tempted by homosexual pornography. Once in a while a passing thought reminds him that he cannot become complacent in his new life, but he's happily heterosexual now, enjoying the love of a wonderful wife."

Sometimes God transforms a life through your care.

Quickscan
HOMOSEXUALITY

Immediate concerns:
1. It's not unusual for a homosexual in crisis to be suicidal. Take threats seriously.
2. Most will be skittish and reticent to talk or give information. Initially, an understanding, noncondemning attitude will likely be necessary to maintain a helping relationship. Your manner will be read minutely.

Keep in mind:
1. Homosexual orientation and behavior is a complex, painful problem. Success rates are not good. This will likely be a wrenching, difficult, and long process.
2. Unless the homosexual wants to change, little you do will help. Let them take the initiative for contacting you and making appointments, and keep them retaining responsibility for their behavior, as much as possible.
3. Few homosexuals consider their preference chosen. Whatever the inception of homosexuality, they experience it as something they *are* rather than something they choose.
4. Homosexuals have learned to expect revulsion, fear, and rejection from the heterosexual population. They need to experience genuine love more than they need condemnation or browbeating.

Things to do or say:
1. Listen, empathize, draw out, show concern.
2. Give them hope in Jesus Christ. God does not want them to be deceived, and he can make them whole and free.
3. Value them as people and build their good points, even when you cannot agree with their life choices.

4. Bring to bear all the written and human resources you can muster. Referral to experts is highly advised.

Things not to do or say:
1. Do not "rescue" them from all the consequences of their behaviors. They may need to feel the drastic sting of crisis to be pushed to a point of change.
2. Do not condemn them or heap scorn on them. They already dislike themselves and are trying to cope with low self-image.
3. Do not waver about the sinfulness of homosexual practices. You do them no favor by encouraging them to continue in sin, even when the alternatives appear full of difficulty and heartache.
4. Do not promise confidentiality you cannot keep. Others may need to know about the homosexuality or be protected from its path.
5. Do not reveal someone's homosexuality without compelling reasons, and then only to those who must know.
6. Never make light of the homosexual's plight through jokes or ill-chosen words.

For further study:
Moberly, Elizabeth R. *Homosexuality: A New Christian Ethic.* Greenwood, S. C.: Attic Press, 1983.

Payne, Leanne. *The Broken Image.* Westchester, Ill.: Cornerstone Books, 1981.

Payne, Leanne. *Crisis in Masculinity.* Westchester, Ill.: Crossway Books, 1985.

Saia, Michael R. *Counseling the Homosexual.* Minneapolis: Bethany House Publishers, 1988.

Van den Aardweg, Gerard. *Homosexuality and Hope.* Ann Arbor, Mich.: Servant Books, 1985.

Wilson, Earl D. *Counseling and Homosexuality.* Waco, Tex.: Word Books, 1988.

SEVEN

MAJOR ILLNESSES AND INJURIES

It requires more courage to suffer than to die.

NAPOLEON BONAPARTE

Life can seem capricious:

- A lively young woman hops into the car to run an errand. Four minutes later she's dazed and injured, looking into the anxious eyes of rescuers from a pile of twisted metal and broken glass.
- A gray-flannel-clad executive clutches his chest and falls to the city street amid the litter — a victim of a heart attack.
- A rambunctious high school linebacker lowers his head to spear a ball carrier — and spends the next year immobilized and the rest of his life a quadriplegic.
- A new bride develops weakness in her legs and then goes suddenly blind. Extensive tests determine multiple sclerosis the culprit.

Each event was unexpected, unwanted, a crisis. Into these experiences pastors are called.

Sudden Incapacitation

Medical considerations. When injury or disease strikes, medical attention must be the first concern. Writes Eugene Kennedy, professor of psychology at Chicago's Loyola University, in *Crisis Counseling,* "The first common-sense rule, echoed in cliches like 'stand back' or 'give them air,' is the priority of getting adequate medical attention before achieving any other goal. One may be more inclined to handle the emotional aspects of the problem, but this is surely secondary when one is involved in an obvious physical emergency."

At the early stage of trauma, emotions enter in mainly in the realm of hope, the will to survive. Any physician can tell of people who gave up the will to live and died of injuries or illnesses they could have conquered. They will also tell of people who through pure grit and determination beat the odds and survived. The determining factor: the will to live.

How is the will to live encouraged? By giving a reason to live, and that can be communicated by love, family support, reminders of life beyond the trauma. Touch communicates care. Visions of the future give something to push toward. "I think of what *I'm* excited about living for," says one helper, "and that helps me remember what may motivate them."

How, then, is the will to live dampened? LOOSE LIPS SINK SHIPS was the poster motto from the Second World War. The same poster belongs in the hospital. "As events move along, it's important to avoid making pessimistic observations about the individual's condition, even if he or she seems to be unconscious," writes Kennedy. "Saying how bad things are, or how much worse they might get, is no help to anyone during such a critical time." Of the senses, hearing and touch are usually the last to be lost.

Isolation — the sense that no one shares the distress, no one familiar is around — affects the will. Unremitting pain saps life from victims, as does a sense, real or imagined, of nothing better in the future, nothing to live *for.* Dreadful weariness makes it hard to face an uncertain future. Containing or improving any of these elements adds to the strength of that all-important will to live.

Adjustments. Once a person is stabilized medically, he or she must deal with what often is a radical change in "body image." Glen E. Whitlock describes body image in *Under-*

standing and Coping with Real-Life Crises: "The body is not simply flesh and bones arranged in a unique way. If in one sense a person is more than a body, there is a real sense in which a person's body *is* that person. The only way we recognize people is through their bodies. . . . It is equally true that we perceive *ourselves* as particular bodies. For example, a woman relates to her body not merely as a physical organism, but also as the carrier of her total selfhood. . . . Any change in body image, therefore, involves an altered perception of self. It follows that the more radical the change, the greater the possibility of a radically altered self-perception, and significant changes in self-perception are usually difficult to work out."

One pastor tells of a 45-year-old woman entering the hospital for elective surgery. "She is an active wife and mother, works part time, and lends much time to charities and kids' activities. She's pretty much been able to do what she sets her mind on doing — an achiever. But severe hemorrhaging after two childbirths and continuing internal maladies have taken their toll on her kidney and uterine functions. The doctors agree she needs a total hysterectomy and extensive urinary repair. She expects to be in the hospital a week for the surgery and eight weeks at home for recovery."

Consider the crisis this brings. To this point, her body image might contain these adjectives: active, attractive, reproductive, nurturing, energetic, youthful, competent, care-giving. Think how these adjectives will change from the moment she regains consciousness in the recovery room: painful, weary, immobile, needy, dependent, barren, deprived, apprehensive, limited. She expects full recovery, but a part of her will be missing, and a lot of her energy will be gone. For at least two months, she will have a body telling her different things about herself, and even after recovery, she will deal with an altered self-image.

Pastors try to help such a person come to grips with this different body she inhabits and calls *me*. When recovery is full, the pastoral work takes place in the interim — giving encouragement, pointing out progress, standing beside the person in the darkest times, holding a hand, praying, challenging.

When there will be no recovery, the task is more difficult.

Consider the football linebacker paralyzed from an injury. His body image included: quick runner, rugged, star athlete, sexually attractive, dependable, and useful. In the hospital, unable to move a muscle below his neck, totally reliant on others, humiliated by his body being exposed to strangers, what's the linebacker to think about his body image? It has to undergo complete reconstruction, and as Whitlock says, that's difficult.

What's a pastor to do? "Assist the person to understand the map of the suddenly changed world," is how Kennedy puts it. The linebacker needs to hear of his prognosis, as difficult as it will be to take. He needs to know what he can expect, what he has to face, what he might be able to accomplish. He needs encouragement to keep from vegetating, for there are things he can learn to do for himself. He needs counseling to help him through the depression and bitter disappointment his new body image dropped on him. <u>Most of all, he needs someone to listen to him, to hurt with him, to stick with him, to love him, to reassure him of his continuing value and manhood.</u>

Longer-term care will involve physical therapy, training programs, vocational rehabilitation, nursing services, grants for education. Through all these, he may need someone to go with him.

Here pastors can help, but a church is even better. A dozen people or a dedicated few can provide rides, visit, read to him, invite him to activities, stretch him when he needs it, listen. As he adapts to his new world, it helps when that world is peopled by caring Christians.

Loved ones. The family and friends of the incapacitated also need pastors. The family of the woman in the car wreck or of the man with the heart attack will suddenly find the world turned upside down. The husband of the bride with MS faces the prospect of a life far different than what he'd planned. Major illnesses and injuries plunge a wide circle of loved ones into crisis.

"I try to imagine the needs of her family," says the pastor of the woman entering the hospital for the hysterectomy. "Her husband faces possibly losing his wife. Although it isn't probable, you know it's worried him. He will soon have all the responsibilities of the household along with the added care of his wife. He has the immense hospital bill on top of his wife's loss of earnings during her leave of absence. He'll want to help his children through this difficult time, but who will be helping him?

"The children will miss their mother and worry about her. She won't be there to fix lunches or see them off to school. There will be visits to the foreign world of the hospital, where their mother won't be the vivacious one they're used to. Then they'll have her home as an invalid and will have to care for her, a role reversal. They'll need somebody to help them with this readjustment."

Most of the care needed by families involves listening and assisting. They need to express ideas and fears. They may be angry with the person for "doing this to us," but feel terrible about thinking such thoughts. They may question the fates for causing this to happen to their family. They will be overworked and probably overwrought. A loving, listening, caring pastor can help ease this difficult transition, and a supportive church family adept at casserole baking and child chauffeuring will be greatly appreciated. Those who enter crisis to give hope where there is none, correct and well-timed information where it's lacking, support when it's needed, continuity when all else crumbles, and independence when that's possible, are blessed indeed.

Terminal Illness

Some diseases and injuries people simply do not beat. Eventually, one of them will fell every one of us. Those with knowledge of the specific one, we call terminally ill. It's a mixed blessing.

My father died in 1980 of pancreatic cancer. For several

months prior to his death, he wasn't at all well. Heart problems led to coronary bypass surgery, but when he should have been feeling much better after the surgery, he wasn't. Finally, great discomfort and a jaundice-like state forced him back into the hospital. Exploratory surgery confirmed our worst fears: widespread, inoperable cancer. He was given up to six months to live. God mercifully took him within a month.

So for a few weeks, Dad knew he was terminally ill. We all knew it, and it gave us the opportunity to transact some final, hard but satisfying interpersonal business. I remember standing on a sidewalk outside the hospital grasping the hand of my toddler son and holding my infant daughter — his only grandchildren. He wanted to see them, but he didn't want them to remember him looking as he did. He waved jauntily from the hospital window; the children smiled and waved back, not knowing they'd never see Grandpa again. But he got to savor them one last time.

Another day I sat on his hospital bed, although I knew it wasn't good bedside manners. We spoke of many things — mostly good things like fishing trips and my "swinging like a rusty gate" when he taught me how to bat. We laughed. We related as men. He proudly introduced me to a physician as "My son, Doctor Berkley." When the internist started discussing medical technicalities, I had to let him know my doctorate was in ministry, not medicine.

I'm thankful I had that final time with my dad. We didn't talk about death, but we both implied it. Instead, we affirmed each other and our family and how good it was to be father and son. Because we knew of the terminal quality of his illness, we could make sure a day like that happened.

For all the beneficial aspects of knowing, there are also drawbacks. Seeing my father weakened, dependent, and fading was not easy. Realizing that berserk cells were that minute multiplying and taking life from the one who had given me life was disquieting. None of us likes to see a loved one weaken and die, so in that respect terminal disease is terribly hard. Bit by bit, death wrenches first health and then life from the one we love, and we can do nothing.

But my acclimatizing to the notion was nothing compared to my father's. I would have to learn to live without him; he would soon not be living. I worried about my mother; he felt as if he were abandoning her. I didn't like to see him in pain; he had to bear it. I had to face the notion of death; he stared the reality face to grim face.

How thankful I was for the loving and competent care of my parents' pastor, Ted! He helped my mother and father face the dragon because he stood beside them all the way. He called on them regularly. He prayed with them. He talked with them. He wasn't full of cheap answers, but costly grace. That's the role of pastor in terminal crises.

Terminal Care

How do you break the news of impending death? Or even more basic, *should* you tell a person he's dying? Two words enter in at this point: *hope* and *honesty*. For the critically ill or injured, hope is a vital ingredient for recovery. Kennedy writes, "Study after study has revealed that those patients whose hope is destroyed also do worst in dealing with their injuries or other illness. It is the vital stuff, the 'right stuff' indeed, at a time of physical danger."

On the other hand, many illnesses have almost certain outcomes. Barring a miracle, my father was not going to recover from pancreatic cancer. A leukemia victim in the final stages of the disease will likely not recover. People such as these have exercised a vast amount of hope, and now the time comes for honesty — our honesty with them, and their honesty with themselves.

Kennedy asks: "Suppose the person asks directly whether he or she is dying? This is by no means an unusual question, and it is not one to which we could respond with a lie or a major distortion of the facts. If, in fact, the person is dying, one can say 'Yes,' but not in the tones of a tolling bell. . . . It can be uttered in the tones of one who is sticking with the patient or the victim and who will remain there to fight it out as long as possible."

The terminal patient commonly senses abandonment. From entering the hospital, she ceases being a sentient adult with a personality and becomes a number. Bodily functions of pulse and blood pressure and elimination become more important than a preference for strangers to call her "Mrs. Jones" rather than "Barbara" or "Honey." People are making decisions for her, and she may have little or no say in her own treatment.

H. Norman Wright lists in *Crisis Counseling* four ways abandonment occurs: Communicating in brief and formal monologues, in which those around the patient do nearly all the talking and never allow the person to express inner fears and hurts; treating the person as a nonperson by talking about him as if he weren't there; ignoring or rejecting times when the patient approaches the subject of death, or papering them over with vacuous statements like, "Oh, you don't want to think that"; and literal abandonment, in which people avoid the patient or narrow contacts to the perfunctory.

The great need is to free the terminally ill person to talk about his or her needs and fears, to express those things that shouldn't have to be borne alone. This is where a pastor, secure about the realities of life and death, can open a door for a lonely and sometimes isolated person.

Hospitalized Children

When injury or sickness befalls a child, emotions crank up a few more notches. About eighteen months ago our daughter showed signs of what *might* be leukemia. Twenty-four hours later, test results indicated our fears were unfounded, but those twenty-four hours were difficult. The crisis of gravely sick or injured children reaches the hearts of everyone involved.

While hospitalization of a child proves critical for the adults involved, it may not be as terrible for the child as we might believe. Children are amazingly resilient. R. Wayne Willis, chaplain at Kosair Children's Hospital in Louisville, writes in a chapter of *When Children Suffer*, edited by Andrew D. Lester: "Much recent research indicates that stressors early in a child's life, such as a hospitalization, are not predictive of long-term problems." He feels that how the child responds to stress is more important in determining effects, good or bad, than the mere occurrence of stress.

But children entertain misconceptions about what is going on. They are apt to see the illness as something to punish them for some real or imaginary wrongdoing. This way of looking at it is called the "contamination theory"; something enters from the outside to contaminate them. Older children are able to understand that sometimes bodies break down.

Children need help to place blame where it belongs. They often have to be persuaded to believe the medical problem isn't because they've been naughty. A pastor, equipped with the truth of the Word and the benevolent authority of one close to God, can often help a child set straight his misguided thinking.

Ministering to hospitalized kids takes an understanding of their world. Drawing on the school-aged child's need to gain mastery over the world around him, Willis seeks "to find ways to help that child leave the hospital feeling like a success and not a failure. . . . One way . . . is to invite the child to become your teacher, to teach you what it is like to be sick. I recommend to pastoral visitors that they assume the posture of a student when they visit and in some way convey to the child, 'You are the expert here. I have no idea what it is like to be where you are. Please teach me.' " That sets up the child to be the authority, and everyone likes to feel important, especially in a depersonalized setting.

Willis encourages hospitalized children to take periodic flights of fantasy in the role of hero. Telling them stories of Little Orphan Annie or Huck Finn or Princess Leia or the Karate Kid, he gives them models and challenges them to take on evil and beat it with good. Such tales play up the will to fight, to overcome.

Willis remembers what he wants to do in a child's hospital

room with an acrostic he devised: N-ABLE — name, absolve, bless, lay on hands, and emote. Let's examine these five tasks of the visiting pastor.

Name means to use the child's preferred name, to never treat the child as just another case. Children grow used to being the tummy that hurts, the blood pressure that needs taking, the crying that must be stopped. They want to be Pete or Katherine — their preferred names, better even than Peter or Kathy — not "that hernia case" or "Jim and Debbie's child." Willis encourages speaking even to the comatose and using their names, for many times they can hear.

To *absolve* is to disentangle a child from irrational guilt and to release him or her from true guilt. Ask children why they are in the hospital, and they may reply, "I fell off my bicycle" or "Our house caught on fire." They see the cause-and-effect relationship of accidents. But children admitted for illness may say, "I don't know," and hold some vague notion that it's their fault. Willis asks questions such as, "Do you think you deserved this? Is God trying to get you?" Answers tell him if he needs to tell the child clearly that the illness is not a punishment.

In cases where the child was responsible for an accident, say from riding a bicycle in a reckless way, Willis will "hear a confession" and then say, "Because you have confessed your fault, God has completely forgiven you, and you must now forgive yourself."

Bless is the next step. In *When Children Suffer*, Willis tells of a boy in a burn unit who received a policeman's recently granted Medal of Valor because the officer told him he deserved it more than himself. That was a blessing, an affirmation that boosted the boy. Willis writes, "When a child is meeting the threat of hospitalization successfully, I may say, 'Justin, because of your bravery in the face of great danger, I now dub you David the Giant Killer. From this day forward, you shall be known throughout the land not as Justin Phillips but as David, slayer of giants' — a metaphor, of course, for besting the rigors of hospital life."

Lay on hands. Touch can be a touchy thing. Willis notes that he never met a kid who likes to be patted on the head. He advises entering the child's private space by invitation only.

However, touch is one way of establishing emotional contact. Willis tells of a boy left quadriplegic by a car accident: "Every time I see him, in pretense of brushing the hair away, I make a point to touch his forehead. That is the only contact his sense of touch has with the rest of humanity. His friends have told me he likes it. Some children will enjoy thumb wrestling. Some will let you hold their hand or will take your arm while on a walk. Some will 'give you five' at the end of your visit, older kids a 'high five.' " Pastors take whatever opportunity is granted to lay on hands.

Emote. "The hospital minister's 'territory' is morale, the spirit of the patient," Willis writes. A child is like an adult in at least one way: he needs to talk about his emotional response to all that's happening to and around him. Willis suggests asking feeling questions: Were you scared? Did that make you a little embarrassed? How did you feel when the doctor told you that? To set the atmosphere, Willis isn't afraid to tell stories that show he has been scared or done dumb things or gotten angry.

"Working around honest children has a way of reminding us that there is a little child in each of us that has been stilled through the years of acculturation," Willis observes, "and we may need to spend some time getting back in shape for pediatrics. That means exercising the right hemisphere of our brains, our childlike, creative, playful, imaginative, intuitive self."

To make a child a victor upon emerging from the hospital — that's the goal. Disease or injury may inflict grievous tolls, but the spirit of the child can conquer, especially if that child and his family have the supportive care of pastor and church. With that care, the crisis eventually fades, but the lessons learned — and the faith found — continue.

Quickscan
MAJOR ILLNESSES AND INJURIES

Immediate concerns:
1. Allow the medical personnel to do their work unimpeded.
2. The shock of sudden illness or injury affects not only the patient but all those around him or her. If you can't get to the patient immediately, minister to the family.
3. Timing is important; get to the people as quickly as possible.

Keep in mind:
1. People with terminal diseases probably know it. Our failure to talk about it doesn't shelter them; it isolates them. Whether now or later, they need to talk about it.
2. The adjustment to a new (and often inferior) body image can be a great crisis for illness or injury victims.
3. People need to grieve their losses or approaching death. The five stages of grief — denial and isolation, anger, bargaining, depression, and acceptance — can be expected in both patient and loved ones. These are normal, acceptable, and even therapeutic.
4. Hospitalized children need opportunities to be victors over the oppressors of pain, loneliness, and fear, to be recognized for little victories and significant steps.
5. With children, although hospitalization is traumatizing, it often is no indicator of future emotional difficulties.

Things to do or say:
1. Provide emotional and social support for the hospitalized and their families. Transportation, meals, baby-sitting, companionship, help with bills — all are part of the crisis response of caring churches.
2. Help patients sort the probable results of their injury or illness from the irrational or overstated fears, and then help them decide how to cope with impairment.
3. Give patients human touch, control over their situation,

someone to talk with about what *they* want to talk about, the sense of being important.

4. Offer realistic hope. Help build the will to live.

5. Listen to the person who is ready to talk about death. Help her put life and faith in order so that death becomes a natural transition to real life, not a dread doorway to terror.

Things not to do or say:

1. Do not normally withhold information from the patient. In extreme circumstances (for instance, a car accident where a family is killed except for a lone member fighting for life) it may be prudent to time the release of all the details, but normally people have the right and the need to know the facts.

2. Do not make light of the adjustments an injured person may have to make to a new body image.

3. Do not talk about a patient in his presence — even one in a coma — as if the person were not there.

4. Do not give patients a sense of abandonment. Let them know when they can expect to see you, and make every effort to visit regularly.

For further study:

Kennedy, Eugene. *Crisis Counseling: The Essential Guide for Nonprofessional Counselors.* New York: Continuum Publishing Company, 1981.

Kübler-Ross, Elisabeth. *On Death and Dying.* New York: Macmillan Publishing Company, Inc., 1969.

Lester, Andrew D. *Pastoral Care with Children in Crisis.* Philadelphia: Westminster/John Knox Press, 1985.

Lester, Andrew D., ed. *When Children Suffer: A Sourcebook for Ministry with Children in Crisis.* Philadelphia: Westminster/John Knox Press, 1987.

DEATH OF A CHILD

How strange it is to know that she is at peace and all is well, and yet be so sorrowful!

MARTIN LUTHER
(following the death of his daughter Lena)

Children aren't supposed to die. Old people, maybe, or the infirm. But children — they're supposed to run and play and giggle and *live!*

But we live in a world where accidents and leukemia and other forms of deadly violence wrench children from the arms of their loved ones and leave those arms empty and aching. Few crises so torment the emotions as the death of a child.

Cinda Warner Gorman, associate pastor at Fletcher Hills Presbyterian Church in El Cajon, California, tells of her experience:

The phone rang one evening. "This is Dr. Steele," the voice said. "I'm at the emergency room at Grossmont Hospital with the Meeker family. Jarrett hanged himself on a back yard swing this afternoon. They've pronounced him dead. We need you or Steve here."

Those brief, confusing words would mark the beginning of one of the most intense weeks of ministry I hope ever to experience. My husband, Steve, also a pastor, had already left for an evening meeting. That left me to find someone to watch our children before I dashed to the hospital.

The Meeker family recently had started attending our church, and Jarrett had participated in the boys' choir and Sunday school. But I was having difficulty putting names and faces together as I drove to the hospital. I came into their lives basically as a stranger. In the poorly ventilated hospital conference room that made us choose between suffocation and privacy, we began to share the difficult week and months ahead.

I listened in as the deputy coroner obtained the information for his report: Jarrett had come home from choir practice and was playing in the back yard while his sister napped. His mom, Judy, had asked him to stop throwing rocks, so he began to swing on a nylon rope suspended from a eucalyptus tree. The rope was knotted at the bottom for a foothold, but a section above the knot had unwoven, creating a loop.

Judy had gone into the house to answer the phone. When she had come back outside, she felt the silence. Looking around, she discovered Jarrett hanging from the loop in the rope.

She pulled him out and ran into the house to dial for help. Then she carried him into the front yard and continued her efforts to revive him there so the paramedics could find her quickly. But it was too late. Despite lengthy procedures at the trauma ward, nothing would revive Jarrett.

Down the hall from our "scream room," Jarrett's body lay in blanket-covered repose. In our stuffy confines, Jarrett's dad, Keith, sat stunned on a couch with Judy. Dr. Steele, the physician who had called me, was with us. He had been Jarrett's godfather.

Plain talk was my first, halting technique. The parents needed to talk about Jarrett. Our initial conversation focused on Jarrett's gregarious, friendly style with other children, his learning difficulties that were showing improvement, and his love for God's creation.

Eventually we journeyed to the trauma room, where Jarrett's body lay covered like that of a sleeping child. I encouraged his parents to stroke his face and hair. Like any mother, Judy commented on his dirty socks.

As the grandparents and aunt and uncle arrived, I found ministry to be hugging the sobbing father and providing tissues. Through her tears, Judy shared her concern over telling the younger daughter this tragic news. I discouraged the use of metaphors about "sleep" or "God needing Jarrett" because these are so easily misinterpreted. When I offered to be a part of the initial conversation with their daughter, Judy and Keith seemed relieved.

Talk turned to the idea of a memorial gift in Jarrett's name. We hit upon the idea of establishing a program for needy children to attend Zoo School at the San Diego Zoo. The family knew it was something Jarrett had enjoyed, and they wanted to open it up to other children. We designated the church Deacons' Fund as a collection point, and that simplified the details for a few weeks.

Our early discussion also included options for burial or cremation. It was important that this be their decision and one that was mutually agreed upon. They decided they'd involve their daughter in the process of finding a burial site as one way of including her in the coming days.

Pastoral ministry in this crisis also included returning with the family to the scene of the accident — their home. By now my husband had arrived at the hospital, and he took over this next stage. We exchanged a few words of information in the hall and prayed with the family again. Then I left, assuring the family I'd return in the morning to share the news with Jennifer.

Early in the morning the school principal responded to my phone message. We discussed the details of the accident so she could share it factually with the school counselor and teachers. I suggested the word *hanging* be avoided since the connotation would be that it had happened on purpose. Visiting the school later that morning, I was pleased with the sensitive presentations being made to each grade level. Teachers used the words *accidentally strangled* to describe what happened.

Most books about explaining death to children will tell you 5-year-olds have a limited concept of the finality of death. This was not the case with Jenny. Cradled in her mother's lap on the bedroom floor, she alternated between tears and perceptive observations. "Jarrett never got to grow old and be a grandpa" indicated to me that she knew Jarrett was not going to come back. "I wish I could just wake up and this would all be a bad dream" meant that this was reality for Jennifer.

We talked about the nature of accidents and about Jarrett's body still being at the hospital but that it would be buried in the coming days. (While it was not the case in this situation, some children take discussion of *bodies* to mean that the head is not included. Children are literal in their understanding.)

We assured Jenny that she could express a full range of feelings even though there would be many sad people around in the coming days. Jenny later told her mother that "Pastor Gorman said I could laugh and play or be quiet and show sadness and tears, and it was all okay."

While we chose Jenny's bedroom for this conversation for the sake of privacy, it was probably a mistake. Her subsequent dreams about things on the walls and dressers might have been because we shared such bad news in a place she called her own.

In planning the memorial service with Jenny's parents that morning, we scheduled it for a time that could include classmates and teachers. We decided to use taped music of the boys' choir. There would be a children's sermon, and friends would be invited to share good memories of Jarrett. Keith and Judy prepared a display of Jarrett's models and baseball cards.

About 350 people attended the memorial service, eighty of whom were children who crowded the chancel for the children's sermon. Using two stuffed caterpillar/butterflies, I created a story about their discussion of what it would be like to fly. One crawled into a cocoon (a paper bag large enough for the butterfly's wings to unzip) and came out a butterfly. But he couldn't come back and tell his friend what flying was like. It was beyond any description a caterpillar would understand. "Jarrett can't come back from heaven to tell us how wonderful it is to live there, either," I concluded, "but we know it is a happy, exciting experience for him."

Later Judy told me she had too little time "alone with Jarrett" at the funeral home. Now I would stress the importance of such time and suggest visitation by others be scheduled at another time. The least we can do is provide sufficient opportunity to be with a dead child.

Pastoral Concerns

Pastor Gorman's experience illustrates several pastoral concerns. First, most families who have just lost a child will be in shock. Their ability to make decisions and think straight, even to find their way into the next room, will likely be impaired.

Gorman took the initiative. She talked with the family, assessing their mental state and bringing comfort. She saw to it that they went into the room where their son lay, allowing them the opportunity to experience death's reality.

Second, she or her husband accompanied them as they performed many of the little tasks that seem so monumental when grief has shut down one's ability to cope. Steve went home with the family. Cinda helped them tell Jenny. Cinda went by the school.

You'll notice what she *didn't* do. She didn't answer all their questions or try to fix everything for the family, as if anyone could. Rather she slipped quietly and competently into the situation, offering her assistance and counsel as needed.

More than anything else, Gorman was a loving presence — someone entering into the family's grief from a caring and compassionate standpoint, someone personifying the Holy Spirit standing alongside (*parakaleo*) the grief stricken. Her memorial service message to the children offered hope and joy. Her suggestion for the memorial gift gave an opportunity to wrest some good out of a bitter experience.

Chaplain Wayne Willis of Louisville's Kosair Children's Hospital finds himself the paraclete with brutal regularity. Many times he takes his place on the emergency team. His role: to care for the relatives.

"When I'm called to the emergency room," he says, "my objectives are fairly limited. First, I try to discover as quickly as possible all I can about the dead child and the circumstances — How old is the victim? Who is at the hospital, and what is their relationship to the deceased? How much do they know? Were good-bys said? Is the body mutilated? Was the death instant or was there great pain? These and other bits of information help me deal with the family."

In the frantic activity of the emergency room, Willis explains, the staff expects the chaplain to "take care of the family." Doctors and nurses have their hands full starting IVs and opening airways. Those who arrive with the victim — sometimes up to a couple dozen — are shunted off to a waiting room. They don't know what's happening or what to expect.

When the patient is finally pronounced dead, staff members aren't eager to face the family. They often feel a little angry or defeated or guilty. That's where the clergyperson can step in.

"At this point, I can be helpful," Willis cautions, "but, of course, I'm not going to be able to make everything all right. My job is to do what it takes to 'get them through the night.' After all, what wise things can I say? Nothing. Their child is dead. That won't go away no matter what I say. So I try to give them the information they need, encourage a full catharsis, and help them wade through the many things that have to be done."

When the responsibility is his to inform the family of the death, he tries to make it simple and direct. According to Willis, "It's important to use the word *dead* or *death* when I tell the family. In a hospital, where medical professionals have difficulty accepting death, it's easy for the family to deny death's reality. So I tell them gently but directly, 'I'm sorry, but your child has died.' "

Then he walks the family through the various activities that accompany death: discussing the question of an autopsy, deciding on which funeral home to call, helping them make calls to others who need to be informed, securing the child's personal belongings, filling out paperwork. Willis finds it nearly always helpful to encourage the family to view the body at the hospital after the tubes are removed and blood and others signs of trauma have been cleaned up. Rituals such as these nudge the family toward good grieving by saying in effect, "This child is really and finally dead."

Clear, specific communication is needed: "Let me take you to the telephone." "I'd be happy to dial for you." "Tell me whom to contact to take you home." People are reassured that someone is in charge and knows what to do.

The specific *pastoral* role is a subtle one. Even the pastor's presence as one representing God can evoke both positive and negative responses. Chaplain Willis tells of one particularly memorable experience:

"A little boy struck by a car was rushed to our hospital. When I arrived I could tell the boy wasn't going to make it, although they were still trying their best to revive him. The family was in a waiting room by themselves. Nobody was talking. They just sat there, each in separate, shocked grief. Even the air in the room seemed to be waiting for the inevitable death notice.

"I relayed to them what factual information I knew and went out of the room every ten minutes or so to get an update. But as I talked with several of the people, the father never said a word. He was a mountain of a man, and he sat still as death itself, hardly blinking an eye.

"Finally a doctor entered the room and said the boy had died. At that, the father bolted upright to his full six-foot-plus height. He clenched his fists and began striding across the room straight for me. I braced, waiting for my lights to go out.

"He got about halfway across the room and stopped. He screamed at the top of his lungs, 'Where's your precious God?!' Then he collapsed to the floor and sobbed the deepest sobs I've ever heard.

"I was relieved to be safe, but for a moment I honestly felt guilty as charged for being a stand-in for God, for having no answers about why little children get run over by cars. That day, part of my ministry was to serve as a lightning rod to discharge the anger and bitterness that grieving father had to let out. I'm not supposed to take such emotion-charged statements personally. They're not meant for me. They're a natural reaction to the shock of bereavement, to what life has dealt. Most people move beyond them, as did that father that day."

But not all the God-identifications are negative. Often people find strength and assurance by the mere fact a pastor is with them. It tells them God is with them.

It is often the little kindnesses that parents remember. "People come up to me months, even years, after their child's death and tell me, 'You may not remember me, but one thing stands out vividly from the awful night when our daughter died: your kindness in calling my mother. I just couldn't do it myself,' " Chaplain Willis says. Bringing a cup of cold water, walking a father around the block when he "just has to get out of the hospital," picking up the purse the dazed mother forgot, offering a Kleenex — these simple, caring actions often mean more than a truckload of words. They broadcast: I care, and so does God.

The words a pastor speaks are also important, however. Therefore they must be chosen carefully, no easy task in an emotion-torn situation. "Some people understand 'God language,' " Willis advises, "and with them I have immediate authority." With such parents who share a common faith, pastors can speak of God's love and care, of God's faithfulness, of God's own loss of a child, of God's victory over death. These are great truths every Christian knows and spouts easily before the emotions hit. To make them a solid anchor in the storm of feelings at death is the difficult task of the pastor.

Pastors want to avoid the sense of pat answers and give the message: "It's okay to break down. It's okay to question. It's okay to be angry at death. God's bigger than all these struggles. God will still be there — loving us — when we quiet down and emerge on the other side of this tragedy."

In this age, however, it's not safe to think people understand God or God talk. "Working in a hospital," Chaplain Willis explains, "I've learned to assume a strong faith is missing for most people. They have little theological understanding through which to process this loss. When I feel that is the case, I look for clues to tell me when to talk of God and faith. The most innocuous opening I've found is to ask with a quizzical voice, 'Would there be any kind of religious tradition you come out of?' The quizzical tone tells them I don't assume anything, and the question allows them to tell of a faithful grandparent or parent, even if they themselves have no operating beliefs. How they answer gives me clues on how to proceed.

"For those with some kind of faith history, I may ask, 'How do you fit God into all this?' That allows the opportunity to rail against the 'unfairness,' express the comfort they receive from God, ask questions that have them knotted inside, or work through any number of other thoughts and feelings. At this point, I become more than a kind person; I can minister as a Christian pastor."

Willis, however, finds some people braced against him for the very reason he is a pastor. "People are suspicious," he sighs. "If they have a negative idea of 'preachers' or 'religious folk,' this is one time they're not going to disguise it. If they want to remain distant, or if they don't want to talk, I resort to the role of a caring hospital staff person. They can use the cup of cold water, too, and it will probably do more good than any number of forced words."

Helping Others through Grief

Siblings, grandparents, other relatives, friends, and classmates also feel the loss. While focusing on the parents, it's easy to forget the help these other people need.

Chaplain Willis expressed an interesting insight: "Grandparents grieve doubly." Grandparents become deeply attached to their grandchildren. In them they see the future of their line. They don't expect to bury their children, much less their grandchildren. The incongruity of it all adds to the suffering.

On top of that, grandparents hate to see their children, the parents, suffer. The pain of the parents hurts those who are *their* parents.

Pastors cannot take that load away, but even recognizing it can help the grandparents, who may not understand all they're feeling. Including them in the events and care following the death helps them with their grief. If they minister to their children, that can be therapeutic for both generations.

Pastor Gorman had both a sibling and a group of school and church friends to inform about the boy's accidental death. Working with the parents, she had many questions to answer: What would be the best setting for telling the sister? How should we phrase it to cause the least harm? Should she see the body? When? Should she go to the funeral? How should classmates and church friends be notified? What kind of service or remembrance will be best for them? How will we deal with their questions or fears?

Gorman chose to talk with the sister after a good night's sleep and in daylight, in the comforting surroundings of her room with her family there. They wanted her to feel the security of family and familiar places at the time she was to be shocked with the news of loss.

In hindsight, the family probably would have chosen a setting other than the girl's bedroom. They feel it has become associated to some extent with the bad news. They do feel good, however, about the way they told her and the sense of security that surrounded her at a time when insecurity would be sprung on her.

School counselors prepared Jarrett's classmates to understand his death. Since the counselors weren't outsiders, they could more effectively work with the children. Gorman's presence at school did prove comforting to those who knew her from her church.

Sudden vs. Prolonged Death

For many years Chaplain Willis coordinated a self-help group for grieving parents. In those sessions, he often heard parents who lost a child suddenly reach out to those whose child's death was lingering. "How could you ever stand watching your child's life slip away little by little?" they ask. "We can't imagine how painful that would be. We'd never be able to stand the sorrow!"

The other parents reply, "But we can't fathom how terrible it would be never to have the chance to say good-by, never to 'finish your business' with your child. At least we got to do some special things like go to the Rose Parade or buy our child a stuffed toy. We can't imagine losing our child in an instant; the pain must be awful."

The reality of loss is the same in both instances, but the dynamics accompanying it differ. Parents whose children died lingering deaths from leukemia or congenital heart problems have a wide and growing range of resources to help them: Ronald McDonald Houses, pediatric hospice programs, and such charities as Dream Factory that provide dying children one last wish, such as a trip to Disney World. But parents have to come to grips with their inability to alter the course of the disease. They have to support that child emotionally, take care of their regular workday duties, bear the burden of staggering hospital costs, and watch their worst nightmare in slow motion.

Parents shocked by the sudden death of a child suffer different concerns. Often a sense of real or false guilt accompanies the death: What if I hadn't let him have the car? What if I'd seen her on the patio before she fell in the pool? What if I'd insisted on her staying in her car seat?

The week before I talked with Chaplain Willis, he'd seen three sets of bereaved parents. One child died by crib death. The unspoken feeling of that child's parents was, *What kind of rotten parent am I for sleeping while my son was dying?* Illogical, unreasonable, but so very real.

Another toddler drowned. While dad was in the shower and mom was distracted by TV, he shot out of the house unnoticed. Within five minutes the family was searching for him. Thirty minutes later he was found in a pool six houses away. He couldn't be resuscitated. What do the parents feel? Guilt. *How could we be so negligent?* Yet it could happen to any parent.

A third child was hit by a car. He was playing with friends in the street. When someone yelled "Car!" he jumped into its path rather than to safety. His parents' haunting question: *Should we have let him play without supervision?* He was old enough. He just made one very bad mistake.

"My job is to help parents sort rational from irrational guilt," says Willis. "Sometimes they *are* guilty. In that case I gently have to confirm their guilt and help them work through its consequences. I don't try to take away that guilt. Instead I want to draw it out of them, hear it, help them acknowledge and accept it as scar tissue, and then move them toward forgiving themselves, just as they have to do with any other shortcoming in life." This is where pastors have much to offer the bereaved parents. Forgiveness is Christianity's forte.

Irrational guilt is tough to tackle. It has no cause in reality and no visible solution. Willis suggests direct and repeated statements: "No, it was not your fault that Richie walked to school that day; tens of thousands of excellent parents let their children walk to school. You are not to blame for the freak accident that took his life." And then reinforce it repeatedly, possibly for years. It can be frustrating for the pastor who can't seem to convince the parent. Willis says philosophically, "Some parents seem to need to flagellate themselves as a way of coping."

The lack of closure is the other particular concern of parents facing a sudden loss. They have no chance to say those things that so often go unsaid in the flurry of life: "I love you. I'm proud of you. You bring me joy. I forgive you." A quarrel that wasn't resolved or a resentment never cleared can clog the passages of restoration for a parent.

Reality therapy — repeatedly stating the rational until the parents, irrational in grief, heal enough to understand — is probably the best course. The parents need to concede that some affairs in life never get settled. They will not have the chance to say what they might have said or demonstrate what they didn't do, but a lifetime of parental care doesn't boil down to one piece of unfinished business. The pattern of loving care, set long before, better demonstrates the essence of their parenthood.

Miscarriage and Stillbirth

"Please, don't call it a miscarriage. My baby is dead!" These poignant sentences from a mother who had lost a child before birth sum up the feelings of parents deprived of expected children: they don't want their loss downplayed.

The tendency of those around is to console with words to the effect, "Well, at least it's not as bad as it would have been once you had a chance to hold your child." Not necessarily true. Bonding occurs early. That child in utero is a real child. Hopes and dreams and characteristics become attached to it long before it's born. When that child fails to make a grand entrance, the empty and darkened stage takes a lot of getting used to.

Pastors are wise to treat a miscarriage or stillbirth as they would any other death. The parents and loved ones need to feel free to grieve. For those who have had a difficult time conceiving, this is an especially bitter time, signifying not only the loss of a child but possibly a sense of fundamental failure ever to be parents.

Chaplain Willis advises visiting the parents as soon as possible after the death and evaluating their reaction to the loss, affirming them, and helping them express their grief. Here are some of his guidelines:

"(1) Attend to the father as well as the mother. Sometimes the father's sense of loss is as great if not greater than the mother's. (2) Draw out the story of events and feelings leading to the loss, giving attention to matters likely to bear on the grief process, for example, marriage relationship or lack of it, planned or unplanned conception, normal or problem pregnancy, delivery (Death known before delivery? Normal delivery? Malformation?), and fantasies and fears attending the pregnancy and delivery. (3) Work through the postmortem process: seeing or holding the baby, bathing and dressing it, deciding on an autopsy, making burial or funeral plans, naming, taking pictures, retaining keepsakes such as a footprint or a lock of hair. (4) Discern the parents' interpretation of the cause of death, including their understanding of the medical explanation, their theological or philosophical understanding of it, their sense of personal responsibility, and their blame of themselves or others. (5) Ascertain the quality of their support system: marriage, family, friends, support group, church, therapist, and work colleagues. (6) Give any guidance as indicated, such as how to break the news to other children, how to handle inane comments, how to cope with others' awkward avoidance, and how to handle the anticipated stress on their marriage relationship."

The banal comments they might have to field include: "Don't worry; you can always have another" (Every child is unique; you cannot "replace" anyone); "God wanted another little angel" (That makes light of a tragedy and tends to paint God as a tyrant who toys with our lives); or "I know exactly how you feel" (Nobody can say that honestly).

The pastor's most important care responsibilities: to accept and understand the depth of emotions in the parents and allow them to express them fully, and to encourage anti-denial activities such as holding the child, taking pictures, or naming the baby. While these may accentuate sorrow at the time, they allow the deep wounds to begin to heal.

Your Own Feelings

Cinda Gorman writes, "I've dealt with death frequently, but nothing really prepares one for the sudden death of a child — in this case a child so close to my own children's age. I discovered that among the many needs to be met at such a time were my own."

Perhaps in no other situation do a pastor's feelings so come into play. Many pastors freely admit the toughest call they make or funeral they preach is for the death of a child. They find it so easy to identify with the bereaved parents. When "This could have been *my* kid!" dominates the pastor's mind, *transference* is at work.

Many pastors fear breaking down in front of the family; many have. Chaplain Willis, even after hundreds of episodes, acknowledges his tendency to become emotionally involved, even to break into tears when he's with the parents. "For me," he says, "I know I'm vulnerable when I feel the parents are much like me or when the child reminds me strongly of my own. When I recognize these factors at work, I say to myself, *Uh-oh. This one's getting to me.* Recognizing what's going on helps me be authentic. I may break down with the family, but that's not necessarily bad. I don't need to apologize for feeling what any caring person would feel. It's only when it catches *me* by surprise that it becomes a problem. If I know it may come, I can cry out of empathy without falling apart and becoming a problem." An authentic tear may do more good than any number of words.

Long-term Caring

Once the family is through the immediate crisis of a child's death, a long road lies ahead. As Elisabeth Kübler-Ross and others have observed, grief is a process. One of the best contributions of a pastor is to give permission for that grief to run its course. Although that contribution starts immediately as the pastor allows the grieving parent to express anger or guilt or sadness without censure, it continues long after most people expect the grieving parent to "get a grip on himself and get on with life." Good grief will not be rushed.

After years of supervising the self-help group for bereaved parents, Wayne Willis observed several standard topics they most often brought up with one another. These are fruitful topics for pastors to consider during subsequent care.

The last things. Parents seem to need to relive the time of their child's death, and pastors do well to hear them out, even when the story becomes redundant. Parents tend to judge themselves by whether they were there at the child's last moment. They want to know they gave the last ounce of assurance and warmth to their child. Equally important is access to the child *after* death, even to the point of fighting through hospital staff to get there. In like manner, the people who were present at those last hours are especially important to parents. Willis tells of one woman so touched that her child's physicians came to the funeral home that she had their initials engraved on the child's tombstone.

Anniversaries. The three most important occasions following a death are the child's birthday, Christmas, and the death anniversary. The first of each of these occasions is often the most difficult. A visit, a card, or special care during these times is most appreciated, even several years later.

"The pits." Depression may well accompany grief. Often the first dark bout comes about a month after the death when parents begin to panic because they feel no better: *I was supposed to be over it!* Some of what pastors have to say to these people may sound like bad news: The pits are unavoidable *and* they'll probably get worse before they get better. But there is good news: Things will get better; bouts will eventually become less severe and less frequent. A pastoral call at the one-month mark often uncovers and begins to deal with this particular problem of grief. Should depression get severe, medical attention is necessary.

Restructuring life. Among the messages bereaved parents give each other is this: There are no rights and wrongs about the way you grieve. Everyone has to do it his or her own way. Nearly every parent will adapt to a loss in an individual way.

This is often seen in how the child's room and possessions are handled. Some parents want it cleared out the day of death, unable to bear the thought of being reminded by objects associated with the child. Some seal off the room or leave it exactly as it was — almost a shrine to the child. Others sell the house and move within weeks. Pastors can help parents think through such decisions, but the decisions themselves are best left to the parents, free of censure. At the same time, gentle nudges to do such things as visit the grave or go through the child's things may help parents break a taboo and progress in their grief. The idea is to offer encouragement to parents whose grieving renders them dysfunctional, but at the same time to propose no simplistic timetables or rigid formulae for rebuilding life.

Support systems. Avoidance by friends and acquaintances is a common experience of parents whose children have died. Out of awkwardness or fear of what to say, some people shun the bereaved. Yet this is just when families need the most support. From Willis's experience, the greatest hurt of all is to avoid any reference to the deceased child. One mother told him, "I guess they're afraid I'll break into tears if they mention him. But I *want* to talk about him. Others may go their merry way and in a month forget he ever existed, but I want to keep his memory alive." Mentioning him doesn't cause pain; the pain is there already.

Pastors can perform two services: First, they can spread the word (and model themselves) that the parents need someone to talk to about their dead child. By making it a topic of conversation, they help the grieving parents. Second, they can include the parents in the caring program of the church through deacons' visits, pastoral prayers, small groups, and pastoral calling. Grieving church members will need to walk the valley, but it need not be a lonesome valley. The care of a loving church, exercised over months, can move them beyond the chasms of crisis.

Quickscan
DEATH OF A CHILD (including miscarriage and stillbirth)

Immediate concerns:
1. Get to the parents or arrange for someone to join them.
2. Arrange custodial care for children of the family.
3. Clear your schedule for a number of hours.

Keep in mind:
1. Expect intense grief. Parents may be nearly unable to function, to make decisions, to put one foot in front of the other.
2. Anger may accompany grief. A common response is to be angry at the "injustice" of a child's death. That anger may be displaced at God or God's vicar — you. It is not necessarily a bad sign. Bear it as much as possible.
3. Miscarriages or stillbirths are often experienced as any other death of a child. They are not lesser deaths.
4. The survivors need a loving presence more than answers. Your greatest gift may be a warm touch, a sympathetic tear, an errand run, or your silent company. Family members want factual answers to questions of the child's care or death circumstances, but their deeper, rhetorical questions are for the sake of emotion, not answers.
5. You will not be able to explain away the death or "fix" the situation. Be resigned to walking beside the family rather than trying to raise them above the situation.
6. You will likely be the only clear-thinking party when you are with the grieving. You may have to speak simply, repeat yourself, suggest logical decisions or steps to take, or perform menial tasks for the family.

Things to do or say:
1. Attain factual information from authorities, hospital personnel, and others to keep the family well informed.
2. Find a private place for the family to grieve.
3. Attend to the physical health of family members. Hyperventilating, fainting, and other physical symptoms often

accompany intense grief. Sedation is normally unnecessary and counterproductive.

4. Allow the family to express grief, even expressions that may seem odd or bizarre to you, as long as they are not hurting themselves or anyone or anything else. This speeds healthy mourning.

5. Work the family through the necessary steps after death: disposition of body, identification, retrieval of personal belongings, signing of papers, notification of people.

6. *Be* Christ in their presence. Care, love, accept, and forgive as he would.

7. Return to the family some sense of structure and control, both of which they have lost in the death. Be steady and in command of the situation, but let them make what decisions they can.

Things not to do or say:

1. Do not attempt cheeriness in the face of deep loss. Victory is in Christ, but that message is best heard at a later time.

2. Do not expect family members to act responsibly or rationally.

3. Do not assume that life will return to normal for the family within a few weeks. It will take a long time.

4. Do not attempt to cheer parents after a miscarriage or stillbirth with words that downplay the significance of the death, such as, "You can always have another."

For further study:

Bayly, Joseph. *The Last Thing We Talk About.* Elgin, Ill.: David C. Cook Publishing Co., 1973.

Heavilin, Marilyn Willett. *December's Song.* San Bernardino, Cal.: Here's Life Publishers, 1988.

Kübler-Ross, Elisabeth. *On Death and Dying.* New York: Macmillan Publishing Co., 1969.

NINE

DEATH OF A SPOUSE

Because my grief seems quiet and apart,
Think not for such a reason it is less.
True sorrow makes a silence in the heart,
Joy has its friends, but grief its
  loneliness.

ROBERT NATHAN

"Till death do us part": When the wedding vows are spoken, it might as well read "forever," because death seems but a remote possibility for the young. But *forever* eventually comes, and when it does, the tight knot tied at the wedding is severed, leaving frayed ends in need of binding.

Gone is the dear companion, the keeper of books, the vacation partner, the purchaser of groceries, the maker of dinner, or the fixer of cars. Gone is the one who shares sunsets or midnight diaperings or pet jokes or holiday traditions. Gone. In one final moment, it's all gone, to be replaced by grief, a miserable substitute.

The First Moments

There is no good way to tell someone a spouse has died. Police dread death notices. Doctors hate announcing a failure. Friends feel incapable. That's why the chore often falls on pastors, who dislike it no less than anyone else but have the heart and will to do it anyway.

Several years ago the mayor of Greenwood, Indiana, a

committed member of Community Church, volunteered to fly three missionaries to Chicago in his private plane. At the airstrip he slipped on the tarmac and fell into the path of the propeller. He was killed instantly. Charles Lake, his pastor, was delegated to notify the family.

"In death notices," he says, "I've found it's good to be direct and clear, as well as caring and concerned. I say something like, 'I'm here because your husband has been involved in an accident.' Not mentioning death in the first sentence seems to cushion the blow and allow a split second to prepare. Normally the wife will ask, 'How is he?' suspecting my presence is indicative of the possibility of death. Then I say, 'I'm sorry, but he is dead.'

"I know the next question. Invariably spouses ask, 'Are you sure? It can't be!' The suddenness makes them incredulous. That's why it's necessary to tell them the simple but brutal fact that a loved one is dead. It helps when you have accurate information. Dazed as people become, they still want to know the facts. And the more I can tell them, the better I can help them cope with that first terrible surge of shock and denial.

"Usually people don't know what to do next. This isn't an everyday occurrence for them. They're stunned. At that point I try to help them think clearly, because normally they can't do that alone. Once they have the basic facts, they have a lot of decisions to begin making. As a somewhat detached 'outsider,' I can bring clarity of thought."

Wayne Willis, who works as chaplain at Louisville's Kosair Children's Hospital, mentions that one of the components of grief is often somatic distress: "I've seen people faint, vomit, get splitting headaches, or start hyperventilating upon hearing of a death. Their bodies respond to the shock right along with their emotions. We give hyperventilating people a paper bag to breathe into. When people faint, we lower them to the floor, check pulse and breathing, put something under their head, perhaps cool their brow, and then allow them the few moments to be out cold. Why revive them to the shock? It's merciful to let them stay out.

"We respect physical denial as one way of coping. If someone gets stuck in denial, it becomes harmful, but as an initial response, it's probably necessary."

Willis subscribes to a "let them do what they need to do as long as they aren't hurting anybody" theory of crisis care. That may mean providing quiet presence to a hysterical person or trailing a "bolter." "Some people, when they hear the news of a loved one's death, want to run," Willis advises. "They suddenly feel as constricted in the hospital space as they do in their range of 'solutions' for the death. They need space; they just want to get away from the crowd. I let them go, but I go with them, staying a discreet distance away. These people may need protection, a kind of shepherding, but that can be done by watching them and leaving them alone. I figure I can allow for a little temporary psychosis if it's a way to cope."

When people start screaming or running or fainting or sobbing uncontrollably, it's uncomfortable. That's okay, Willis reminds us. Eventually people will calm down. Right now they probably need the response they have chosen. And a *lack* of response is likely more harmful in the long run. John Milam, my father-in-law, has a saying that puts this into perspective: "It's not normal to act normal in an abnormal situation."

The First Days

The immediate concerns of notification and emotional first aid give way to helping with plans and memorial services and decisions. For the bereaved, life seems a blur of forms to fill out, major decisions to make, and expenses that mount, all when there is little inclination or ability to cope with such an onslaught. Marilyn Willett Heavilin, in *December's Song*, lists a number of activities others can do to help the bereaved:
— Call relatives
— Contact the family attorney
— Locate any existing will
— Call insurance companies
— Locate insurance policies and bank accounts

— Check on existing retirement funds
— Notify Social Security
— Help write the obituary
— Help plan the funeral
— Go with the bereaved to the mortuary and cemetery
— Provide a guest book to use at the bereaved's home
— Find people to provide family meals
— Clean the house
— Mow the lawn
— Grocery shop
— Do minor house and car repairs
— Have someone stay at the home during the funeral
— Have someone record the food and flowers brought to the home

Many of these activities can be covered by friends, family, or members of the church. But pastors often want to be involved in several. Pastor Gary Gulbranson of Glen Ellyn (Illinois) Bible Church takes an active role when he's called into a death situation.

"I try to get to the family as quickly as I can when I hear of a death," Gulbranson says, "and once there, I try to pick up the clues about how I'm needed. It's not my purpose to step in and attempt to control the situation, but to let the emotional state of the spouse dictate my response. Some people need to be taken by the hand and walked through every minute detail. Others seem more in charge and just want someone to accompany them.

"Often I ask if they want me to contact the funeral home. I set up the meeting with the funeral director, and I try to be there unless the spouse objects. The spouse has to make some big decisions about disposition of the body, the expenses of casket and services, and the funeral service. I like to offer my help in putting those decisions in Christian perspective.

"In working with the family, I often hear stories and details about the deceased family member that I can use at the funeral. Sometimes they need help to restructure their memories, so I ask questions to jog their thoughts."

Many pastors sit down with the family during the first

couple of days and get them to reminisce about the deceased member: where the person grew up, how the couple met, where they've lived, special occasions for them, interests and talents of the deceased, interesting family experiences, religious ties, and occasions of Christian significance.

This begins to draw the family together as they remember good times and bad. Sometimes they laugh at a humorous incident. Often tears flow sporadically. People remind each other of cherished times, and one person's memory fills in where another's trails off. The surviving spouse can voice memories and thoughts that will be precious to the children and grandchildren. The whole process can be wonderfully therapeutic, leading toward good grief.

Second, this gives the pastor great material to personalize a memorial service. Many times the pastor, of all those at the funeral, will know the deceased least, and yet he or she is called upon to speak about this near stranger. This time of family reminiscing opens windows into family life and the character and interests of the deceased.

On some occasions the death crisis is complicated by a sharp family disagreement. With nerves on edge anyway, disputes can be unpleasant. "When a family starts fighting — usually over little things — I jump in as an aggressive peacemaker," says Gulbranson. "Sometimes all that's needed is taking charge and saying to the spouse, 'You're the husband (or wife), what do you want?' " Decisions ought to be made by those closest to the deceased. Donnybrooks over items such as costs, who speaks at the funeral, or what kind of casket to buy ought not to be allowed to further disquiet the bereaved spouse or family.

As in any death situation, pastors often will be asked difficult questions: Where was God when my wife was suffering so? With all the bad folks running around, why was my husband the one who died? Why is God silent when I need him? These are difficult at any time, but combined with bitterness or deep emotion, they are all the harder to field.

Quick, glib answers, even when theologically accurate, often alienate the grieving spouse. As Marilyn Heavilin says,

"Few of us are looking for a quick fix. It doesn't take us long to realize that our problem can't be taken care of quickly, and we don't really expect anyone to fix it. What we do need is knowledgeable people around us who will listen and at least discuss our questions with us."

Joseph Bayly experienced the death of three of his children. Listen to what he wrote in *The Last Thing We Talk About* concerning two people who visited him: "I was sitting, torn by grief. Someone came and talked to me of God's dealings, of why it happened, of hope beyond the grave. He talked constantly; he said things I know are true. I was unmoved, except to wish he'd go away. He finally did. Another came and sat beside me. He didn't ask leading questions. He just sat beside me for an hour and more, listened when I said something, answered briefly, prayed simply, left. I was moved. I was comforted. I hated to see him go."

Satisfactory answers to the inevitable questions of death deal more with emotion than substance. Some questions are merely informational: What's heaven like? Why have a funeral? Is it okay to cry? They can be answered briefly and clearly. But no one can adequately answer why a young father dies in an automobile accident that wasn't his fault. When the question is asked by his widow, she needs an arm around her shoulder more than a treatise on the sovereignty of God.

"I treat such questions as rhetorical statements flung into space for the emotional release, not as tests of my theology," one pastor says. "The questioner really needs to hear that God is still there, he does yet care, and, no, we don't really know why things like this happen, but we're sure God feels this suffering as much as we do." Such a response doesn't belittle the deep questioning of a broken heart; it affirms it's *not* bad to ask such questions and comforts the questioner.

In these first days of grief, a pastor can help the widow or widower by serving as an enhanced mirror, reflecting the person's emotions and thoughts with greater clarity and understanding. For example, if a widow says, "I don't know what I'm going to live on now that John's gone," one might reply, "It must feel scary suddenly to have the responsibility for all the bookkeeping when you haven't had it for forty-five years. I think I'd want to ask for some help from a good accountant. We have a couple in the church that I could recommend." Her fuzzy statement of fear is thus heard, analyzed, and echoed back to her in enhanced form, legitimating her anxiety and giving her something to do should she want the help.

"Oh, don't worry. You've got plenty of money!" wouldn't give the same relief. It makes her apprehension sound unwarranted and silly, and it gives her no method to relieve it.

A way to help people voice their feelings is offered by David Seamands. "In situations like these, I often pray using 'we' to express feelings and thoughts the person may not have dared to express out loud for fear they will sound blasphemous. I might pray, 'Lord, we're puzzled by this death, and we wonder sometimes how you fit into it. We know you can do all things, but we wonder why you didn't rescue this loved one. At times it seems unbearable to us, and we even start thinking you don't seem very close when we need you . . .'

"When I grow bold for them in this kind of questioning prayer, people often will burst into tears where before they remained stone-faced. They don't know such prayer is allowable. It doesn't fit the categories of prayer they've seen before. The honesty before God, spoken by someone who represents God, disarms them. Finally they let down and allow their honest emotions and thoughts to show."

By giving grieving spouses a clear picture of what they are feeling, by telling them it's okay to feel that way, by gently pointing to options they can choose, pastors help the bereaved get through those first few days of grief.

The First Months

"Society can be fairly merciless with a grieving person," Chaplain Wayne Willis sighs. "People are given about two weeks, and then they're expected to resume normal activities as if nothing had happened. If they don't get over it soon, some begin to worry about a nervous breakdown or suicide.

Actually it is more like months or even years before many people recover from grief sufficiently even to approach normality."

Many widowed people say the hardest grieving comes after the funeral, after relatives and friends have gone home, after the flowers have wilted and the cards have quit arriving — right when the dreadful drudgery of life without a partner really sinks in. Earlier there was shock, and then a flurry of support. Finally there is only the grinding reality of loss, and grief becomes overwhelming. That easily becomes the crisis within a crisis.

At Grace Lutheran Church in Oconto Falls, Wisconsin, Pastor Kevin Ruffcorn has initiated a program of grief aftercare. It begins at the funeral service, where he lets the family know that likely it will take a year or more to work through their grief. "Occasionally family members make statements like, 'As soon as this funeral's over, we can get on with life,' " Ruffcorn comments. "I have to tell them gently that death affects us longer than a few short days, and if in a month or two they still aren't handling the death very well, if they break down in tears in the grocery store after hearing a song that reminds them of their loved one, that's perfectly normal for good, strong Christians. They're not going crazy or losing their faith. They are just being human."

His second step is a series of phone calls and visits. He stops by a week after the funeral to talk with the widow or widower. This visit, probably after the reality has hit, provides an opportunity for the bereaved to express a new set of grief questions or to rehash the old ones.

"Many times I hear expressions of loneliness," Ruffcorn elaborates, "unbearable evenings without a husband, lonely meals around a table for one, cold beds, and empty houses. I can't take that away, but my call does allow persons to express the grief and to realize that someone understands what they're going through.

"Occasionally I hear soft voices of denial. Donna shared that she often imagined her husband walking through the kitchen door and greeting her with a kiss, just as he always did. I affirm that such struggles are a normal part of grieving and not a sign they are going crazy. I tell them grief doesn't end at the funeral. Yes, they must get on with life, but they also need to feel the wounds of grief before they can heal."

About two weeks later Ruffcorn either drops by or phones, assuring the spouse that he or she remains in his thoughts and prayers. He wants to stress that he is available as a pastor.

"Often this second visit is the watershed," he writes. "Anger and theological questions often appear. One woman mentioned she was having difficulty praying. She was angry and thought the death unfair. As she shared with me, however, she heard in her own words her blame of God. Using Scripture and counsel, I helped her release her anger and understand her feelings. Her devotional life was renewed."

Ruffcorn tries to make a third visit about three to four months after the funeral. "By this time," he notes, "any significant difficulties in the grief process are apparent. Such things as chronic depression or eating or sleeping disorders are signals of problems that go beyond my pastoral skills into physical and psychological realms. In that case, I encourage the individual to seek additional professional help.

"I can, though, help others such as David, whose fiancée was killed in a freak car accident two months before they were to be married. During one visit, David stated he never would be able to love a person again because of his fear of being hurt by loss. His life reflected this attitude as he became more and more a loner. After hours of conversation, David began to see the difficulties of his fearful coping. He's now making cautious steps toward loving again."

As a further step, Ruffcorn enlists the church secretary to obtain the deceased's birthday and anniversary days and mark them on his calendar. He also notes the anniversary of the death. "I make a note to phone the spouse on those special dates because those days are difficult during grief. A phone call from the pastor, no matter how short, conveys the comforting message that someone understands. Around Thanksgiving and Christmas, I also make an effort to call the families of those who died during the year."

One grieving family member understood well the difficulties of the holiday season. "I would like to ask God to cancel December," she said. "We'll try it again some other year." At these difficult times, pastors want to convey support.

But Ruffcorn doesn't shoulder the entire responsibility for grieving spouses. He pairs each new widow or widower with a member of the congregation who has gone through similar circumstances. He asks these volunteers to visit at least every four to six weeks for a year. Their purpose is to be a friend, a listener. They are encouraged to talk about the dead spouse, especially because many others fastidiously avoid the subject. (Grieving spouses almost always *want* to talk about their spouse. They don't want life to go on as if their spouse never existed.) Ruffcorn asks the visitors to contact him if anything comes up that he can clarify or if they have concerns about how the spouse is handling grief.

One writer put it this way: "Pain is an acceptable guest, but not a welcome long-term visitor." The pastor's job is to help move it along at the appropriate time.

Kevin Ruffcorn tells of a day when a Bible study had fallen flat, two committees were going in contrary directions, and a few members had called with "nit-picky" criticisms of one of his pet projects. "It was one of those days when I was beginning to wonder, *Lord, is it worth it?*"

Then the mail arrived. Between frustrations, he tore open a letter and began to read:

Dear Pastor,
Words cannot express my appreciation for your visits. Your presence helped me go through the most difficult struggle I have ever experienced in my life, the death of my husband . . .

"This letter," Ruffcorn says, "reminded me that ministry was taking place and that ministry does take place whenever love is expressed and the effort is made to share the power of the gospel."

Quickscan
DEATH OF A SPOUSE

Immediate concerns:
1. The spouse, if not already notified, needs someone to break the news gently yet clearly.
2. Someone needs to be with the widow or widower. It is never too early for a pastoral call.
3. Help with decisions. In the many that have to be made, your Christian perspective can be useful.

Keep in mind:
1. A newly bereaved person will be in shock. Many manifestations of grief may appear out of control or unseemly. Unless a person is harming someone, however, allow grief to be expressed as it will.
2. Probably the straightest thinker will be you. Help people cope with decisions, plans, and personalities. Take your clues from them as to how much of you they need and want.
3. Angry questions addressed to God are often more felt than meant. The time for orthodox theology will come later. What is needed now is loving care that mirrors God's feelings for the downtrodden. Deal with the emotion, not necessarily the substance, of the questions.
4. Grief takes time to work through. Very likely, things will *not* be okay in a few weeks or even several months. Gently saying this can give the grieving spouse permission to take time to heal.
5. Perhaps the hardest grief will come more than two weeks after the funeral. Grief aftercare is needed.

Things to do or say:
1. Presence often means more than words. Being there, speaking little, touching as appropriate, and praying are the immediate ways to help.

2. Help the bereaved sort the many decisions. Major decisions of finances and lifestyle ought to be postponed. Other decisions, such as burial or funeral arrangements, need immediate thought.

3. Communicate God's care through your care. We cannot always fathom the mind of God, but we can certainly experience the compassion of God's people. In Jesus Christ, God himself knows loss: that's a powerful message.

4. Talk about the deceased. Most people won't. Give the family opportunities to remember.

5. Mobilize the people of the church to share the burden of the bereaved. Visitors (over a period of at least a year), food, household chores, someone to watch the home during the funeral — all are ways to help.

Things not to do or say:

1. Do not stifle the emotions of grief. They need to come out in appropriate ways.

2. Do not give glib answers to the difficult questions of death and loss. Too many words are more harmful than too few.

3. Do not let the funeral be the end of bereavement care.

4. Do not assume a stoic disposition means grief is handled. The lack of emotion can signal overcompensation or denial of grief.

For further study:

Bayly, Joseph. *The Last Thing We Talk About.* Elgin, Ill.: David C. Cook Publishing Co., 1973.

Colgrove, Melba, Harold H. Bloomfield, and Peter McWilliams. *How to Survive the Loss of a Love.* New York: Bantam Books, 1976. (Ignore the plugs for Transcendental Meditation.)

Kübler-Ross, Elisabeth. *On Death and Dying.* New York: Macmillan Publishing Co., 1969.

Lewis, C. S. *A Grief Observed.* New York: Bantam Books, 1976.

SUICIDE

The question of suicide:
  Keep it a question.
    It's not really an answer.

PETER MCWILLIAMS

Suicide intervention is a life-and-death crisis. Bobble it, and we may not get a second chance.

Before he became a pastor, a man we'll call Terry was at work one day when he received a phone call. The caller, Howard, was the 34-year-old son of a fellow worker. Terry knew of Howard's continuing problem with drug abuse, and he remembered that Howard had been hospitalized a while back for psychiatric problems. Howard got right to the point: "Look, I called so you can help my mom. You'll need to talk with her soon, because she's going to find me dead."

What's Terry to do?

Saving a Life

It's remarkable that even most of the suicidal don't want to die. That's why the calls. They're using their next-to-last trick from a bag that's nearly empty. Our task: keeping a precious life intact.

Engagement. The initial moments of the conversation are terribly important. If the caller is absolutely serious about suicide, he controls the interaction. He can hang up abruptly, parcel out or withhold information, get angry and accusing, tantalize, manipulate, or string you along. He can even carry out his intent while you listen.

That's why engaging the caller in conversation is so crucial. Gary Gulbranson, pastor of Glen Ellyn (Illinois) Bible Church, offers advice for this tricky task: "Let the situation play you; don't dominate it. The person calling for help has likely been pushed around by life, pushed to the point of feeling out of control. A suicide attempt is one way to be in charge. When they make that last call, they need to play out their frustrations." So at the beginning of the conversation, Gary doesn't attempt to interrupt them or ask too many questions or argue with their logic. He first listens actively and absorbs their story. That begins to build a bond; the caller feels in some kind of control.

In *Crisis Counseling*, Norm Wright suggests positive statements to build up the caller, such as "You did the right thing by calling," or "I'm glad you called." This can get the caller thinking, *For once I did something right.* It's a small step, but it can both keep the person on the line and begin to rebuild a fractured spirit. The suicidal person is convinced that life is worthless, that probably no one really understands or cares. When into that misperception a warm and caring voice says, "*I* care!" another door is cracked open.

Pastors have a distinct advantage here because Christianity, above all religions, values the individual. Without fingers crossed behind our backs, we can tell *anyone*, "You're a precious child of God, the pinnacle of God's creation."

Inquiry. Once the person appears willing to talk, several items of information will prove greatly helpful. The trick is to charm this information from someone often unwilling to part with it.

If medical necessity doesn't dictate haste, spacing out the questions amid casual conversation is often the best tactic. That way the caller doesn't become edgy from getting the third degree. As much as possible, it's good to ask the questions somewhat offhandedly without giving the feeling you are intent on solving the puzzle so the police can break down the door. What information people won't give directly, they may let slip inadvertently: "You sound a little sleepy. Are you on any medication?"

The most vital information is the seriousness and extent of the suicide threat. Some helpers fear bringing up the word *suicide* when a caller makes vague references about life not being worth living. They don't want to plant the idea. But crisis hotline trainers say that is not the case; the idea will already be there, but the caller may not bring it up for fear of the reaction.

Naming the dragon may well be the first step toward slaying it. Straightforward questions often work best: "Have you ever felt like taking your life?" "When you say you want to 'end it all,' do you mean you're thinking of suicide?" The fact that they can talk to you about suicide without your going to pieces lends an air of stability to their tumbling world.

"Have you already done anything to hurt yourself?" is another logical question. Here specifics are important: What kind of pills, and how many? How long ago? How much blood have you lost? Can you smell gas in the room? These facts ought to be jotted down. They become crucial in short order.

If the person hasn't yet done anything rash, questions center on intentions: If you were to take your life, how would you do it? Have you made any plans? If the answer is to use a gun, even more specific questions follow: Do you have a gun with you? What kind is it? Is it loaded? Do you know how to use it? (This information is also vital for the safety of police officers who may be summoned.) The idea is to find out what steps have been taken to carry out the suicide plan. While pointing out loopholes in a plan wouldn't be advisable, merely talking about the plan doesn't further its course.

The name, phone number, and location of the person calling need to be determined as quickly as possible. But the sense that the helper is after such information may spook some callers. They want to remain anonymous and untraceable.

Some helpers give their name at the beginning of a conversation, and then turn the question naturally to the caller:

"And what's your name?" If it is given, it's a good idea to write it down. If the person balks, counselors can say, "It would be easier if I had a name to call you. Could you give me your first name? I'd feel better if you would."

Discovering the location of the caller is especially important if the person is in danger. If direct questions don't work, indirect ones may shake out bits of information, such as the general area of town, or if the person is at home or in a public place, has people around or not, is nearby or far away. All are facts that may come in handy should direct intervention prove necessary.

Another bit of information you'll want to note is the resources at the caller's disposal. Is anyone nearby who could offer assistance? Is the person emotionally close to family and friends, or is he or she psychologically alone? Are other people contributing factors? Is the person a Christian? What self-understanding is evident? Can the person think straight, or have emotions limited the natural coping mechanisms? Callers often will let facts slip as the trust level builds throughout a conversation.

Appraisal. Gathering the information is more than a stalling tactic. This information determines the action to take.

One of the first considerations is: How urgent is this? A suicide in progress is greatly urgent. A vague reference to "ending it all someday" probably isn't as urgent, although it is serious. Other factors pointing toward urgency include: a valid, specific, and lethal suicide plan; means readily available; agitated depression; a lack of a support system; a history of suicide attempts; and, surprisingly, a sudden turn for the better after a period of melancholy.

Another consideration: What has led to this point? Why is ending it all the only apparent solution? The helper often can identify several options far less drastic than suicide. But because of the accumulation of crises or the fog of depression or the immediacy of upset, the caller has been unable to chart those escape routes.

What is the person's understanding of suicide? As strange

as it may sound, some people don't really understand the finality of suicide. Teenagers may see it mainly as a way "to show them" or to get attention. They don't think beyond the climactic moment to the fact they won't be there to savor it.

It's good gently to probe for the theological understanding of suicide, as well. Do they consider it wrong? What do they think will happen to them after death? Have they even considered the morality of it all? Deeply held moral beliefs, or even fears, may be allies in the push toward life.

Action. The person has called; the suicide attempt is transpiring or at least imminent; the facts are in. That means it's time to act. What can you do?

A drastic strategy: Determine where the person is and get help to him or her immediately and in whatever form necessary, including getting the police involved. This is the course to take when a suicide is in progress or when a lethal and workable plan is likely to be put in effect.

Most of the social rules go out the window at a time like this. The helper may worry about breaking confidence or losing the person's trust by initiating precipitous measures the caller has told the helper not to try. (It's a good idea not to promise complete confidentiality from the start. Promise instead: "I won't do anything to harm you." Many callers will accept that in place of a promise not to tell anyone.) But even if one has promised not to call the police, strict honesty will mean little at the person's funeral. As Gary Gulbranson put it, "You can worry about putting the emotional pieces back together later; you've got to get help now to save a life!"

It's a good pre-emptive strategy to work out a distress signal to bring a secretary or your spouse into the room where you take such calls. Then a hastily jotted note can send them to another phone to have the call traced or to dispatch an emergency team. The universal distress signal — three raps on the wall or loud thumps or buzzes on the intercom — is one way to summon help for you, the helper.

A pretty good strategy: Keep the person talking. As long as the caller stays on the line and talks, chances are the suicide won't take place (unless the attempt has been made and is now taking effect).

Talk is an antidote, healing in itself. Just the fact of another human dropping everything to listen — really *listen* —can dissipate noxious emotions. So talk away. It's a good first strategy.

A better strategy: Obtain some kind of commitment from the caller. After a long, wrenching conversation, it's not uncommon for the caller to feel somewhat indebted to the helper. Or maybe there's a prior attachment that made the person call in the first place. Either of these debts can be used by the helper.

Charles Lake, pastor of Community Church of Greenwood, Indiana, advises, "Make a pact with them and hold them to it. I tell them, 'You know, after all we've been through together, don't you think you owe it to me to at least give me a call before you do anything drastic? Promise me you'll do that one little thing for me.' And they do it. The very fact they feel obligated to call me before they pull the trigger keeps them from following through with their plans. They either call, giving me another chance to stay their course, or they put the gun down. It's an odd sense of duty, but it seems to work."

An even better strategy: Work out a plan. The suicidal person has been working on a suicide plan; now's the time to advance a life plan. It can begin with eliminating tools that would make a distinct suicide plan feasible. That may mean getting someone else to keep the firing mechanism for a gun, purging the house of lethal medications, or disposing of a hose that would attach to the automobile exhaust.

But a life plan goes farther. It helps the caller begin to walk toward life and health. The first steps may be tiny, such as trusting the helper enough to divulge one's name, or scheduling an appointment together in person and promising to keep it. It may encompass a contract to call each other daily or more often if necessary. It may start with a promise to make an appointment with a physician. Sometimes it will involve a step toward Christian faith, such as reading a Christian book or meeting together to discuss being born again. The life plan eventually ought to get more complex, branching into a complete therapeutic program involving health, psychological, and Christian professionals.

An overriding strategy: Prayer. Most people can pray and listen at the same time. Bringing the power of God into the situation is absolutely necessary. It's not right to think, *All I can do is pray*. In reality, it's a case of *the best I can do is pray, and that's a lot!*

Aftercare. Eventually the crisis fades, but people who have once threatened or attempted suicide are at risk to repeat. Many live in a state of low-grade crisis. They need extended care.

Often such care needs to come from mental health professionals. An acutely suicidal person presents high counseling risks. Many times clinical depression is present, and that needs the expert care of physicians able to administer antidepressant medications. (The *physiological* basis of many depressions has been getting much research lately, and several effective prescription medications work to restore depressed people to normal lives. Getting a depressed person to a medical specialist in depression can be one of the most effective ways to help that person.)

Other deep-seated emotional problems also need extended counseling, and most pastors don't hesitate to refer suicidal counselees to competent psychological or psychiatric care. But they then supplement the secular care with the rich resources of the church.

A congregation can provide what family or neighborhood haven't: love and esteem. A church is a place to belong, to be valued, to contribute. Along with medical and psychological care, a suicidal person needs the loving social and spiritual care of a church family. Crisis intervention is complete when the family of faith wraps loving arms of support around a nearly lost member.

All the Right Moves

We left Terry on the phone with Howard, who had made a clear reference to intended suicide. Terry knew the call could terminate suddenly at any point, so he took care to engage Howard in conversation by being warmly diplomatic and not letting his alarm show. He barely knew Howard, so he had little relationship to draw from. He used active listening to gather information.

Howard was, at first, highly agitated: "I don't know why I'm talking to you. I ought to be just doing it. But I wanted you to be able to help my mom. She's going to be really upset, and she'll need your help. Promise me you'll come over here with her after it's all over. Man, will she be freaked out! But that doesn't make any difference to me. I've made up my mind. This is it, baby!"

Terry let him rant. He could hear the rage and confusion crest and subside in Howard's voice. Obviously Howard was ambivalent about living. If he really wanted to die, he wouldn't be spending this time venting his double mindedness and perhaps foiling his plot. Yet the frustration and helplessness were nearly enough to push him over the edge.

"Howard," Terry said with calm warmth, "you sound upset, but I think I can help you. We need to get together and talk this through. How about if I come over to talk? I'd like to help you."

"You're not coming over here! No way. Don't you try. I'm warning you."

"Howard, I wouldn't do *anything* to hurt you. Can you trust me? I want to help."

"Well I just don't want anybody meddling. I only wanted to take care of Mom. She's going to be hurt by this, but it's *my* decision."

"What is this decision you're talking about? Are you considering suicide? Is that what you're telling me?"

"You're darn right I'm talking suicide. I've had it with life, and I don't have to take it any more. I'm checking out of this hole."

Terry needed some vital information quickly, so he took a direct approach. "Howard, what are your plans for 'checking out'?"

"They aren't plans anymore. I've already done it. I took a bunch of pills, and I'm sitting here holding a big, black gun. As soon as we're done — I'm done!"

"Wait a minute, Howard!" Terry warned. "Do you know how final that is? Your life is precious. People care about you. Your mother cares. *I* care! Let's talk about what you're doing." Terry was trying to buy time. He had to keep Howard talking.

While talking with Howard, Terry had gotten the attention of his secretary. When she came over to his desk, Terry scribbled a note asking her to get Howard's mother, Nora. When Nora arrived at his desk, Terry filled her in on the conversation by scratching out notes. Then he wrote, WHERE IS HOWARD? Nora assumed he'd be at his apartment. HOW FAR FROM HERE? About fifteen minutes, Nora thought, and she started to go. CAREFUL, HE'S GOT A GUN! Terry wrote. As Nora rushed out, Terry asked his secretary to call the police and have them meet Nora outside the apartment.

By allowing Howard to vent his anger and by deftly manipulating the conversation to keep him talking, Terry provided Howard a way to do what he really wanted to do that day: get help. Howard calmed down considerably and became less belligerent as time went on. He got a little maudlin. Terry kept him talking. Then, abruptly, Howard said, "Hey, I've got to go."

Terry couldn't let that happen, so he played on Howard's common courtesy. "You can't just hang up on me. That would be rude. I'd like to hear more of what you have to say. I've got all day."

"No, I've got to go. You've been great, but I'm going to hang up now."

"Okay, but would you promise me one thing? Would you

give me your word of honor that you won't use that gun without first calling me back? I want you to promise me just that one little thing. You owe it to me to at least offer that courtesy."

Howard said he wouldn't "do anything else stupid" without first calling back. Then he hung up.

At this point, Terry could concentrate on what had been a third activity behind the phone conversation and urgent notes: prayer.

Nora reached Howard's apartment and found him quietly sitting on the couch. The gun was on a table across the room — loaded and lethal, but unused. Howard told Nora what pills he had taken, and she scooped up the nearly empty baggies as she and paramedics hustled him to the hospital to have his stomach pumped. Terry went to the hospital to offer emotional support to Nora and to begin to minister to Howard.

In the weeks that followed, Terry helped get Howard into a halfway house. Howard got off of drugs and started rebuilding his life. He found a job, began working, and re-entered normal life. Terry met with him several times but realized before long that Howard was out of danger.

A Sadder Task

Not all suicides can be stopped; indeed, not all suicidal people give an indication of their intentions or the opportunity to hinder them. The crisis, then, is for those around them.

The day one pastor we'll call Chad candidated for a new pastorate, a young man slipped out of the worship service about the time Chad got up to preach. The 21-year-old was from a family active in the church. He'd been president of the local Young Life club when he was in high school.

But on this day he went home, wrote several notes, attached a hose to the car's exhaust and ran it into the car in the closed garage, started the ignition, and calmly asphyxiated himself. His parents, on returning from the happy occasion of calling a new pastor, found their son dead in the car.

Chad first heard about it when the church received a phone call from the parents. Since he was the only pastor the church then had, Chad rushed to the people's home, praying for calmness in his spirit and the ability to comfort the family he hardly knew.

At the home, Chad passed the emergency crew ready to wheel the dead boy off to the hospital and met with both parents, deeply in shock. Chad could do nothing about their son's death, so he resolved to provide a loving, helping presence in their time of need.

Before other questions could be asked, somebody had to go to the hospital with the body. Chad accompanied the father and lent support and suggestions as he filled out forms and decided about the disposition of the body and other legal matters.

Back at the home, a woman from the church had arrived. She made it her role simply to sit beside the weeping mother with her arm around her shoulder. A communication far beyond words took place in that simple act. The woman didn't cry. She was just there, caring and mostly silent.

Later Chad counseled with the parents, who naturally were ruminating about why their son would kill himself. "I tried to help them recognize that although their son had made a bad choice, that one choice shouldn't completely define his whole life," Chad recounts. "In the flow of life, we all make many bad choices. His life was made up of many accomplishments and pleasures and good memories as well. I wanted the parents not to dwell on the one fatal mistake he had made."

Those who remain often face problems of guilt, anger, and dreadful loss. They wonder if they might have done anything to prevent the suicide, and often mentally rehearse their actions leading up to the suicide, looking for clues. A sense of rage often accompanies grief: "How could he do this to us! If he weren't dead, I swear I'd kill him myself!" And loved ones face the grief of loss compounded by the circumstances.

The survivors need to talk about their reactions to the suicide. Many acquaintances avoid the subject, if not the survivors, themselves. Pastors offer a tremendous service merely by listening compassionately and validating the survivors' grief.

That's what Chad did for the young man's family. Five years later, healing for that family is still continuing.

Quickscan
SUICIDE

Immediate concerns:
1. If there is any indication of a suicide attempt in process or imminent, call in the police, paramedics, or mental health team, or intervene yourself.
2. Try to determine where the person is as quickly as possible.
3. A suicidal person may be dangerous to others; find out what weapons or other dangers (gas, carbon monoxide) may be present.

Keep in mind:
1. Your primary goal is to keep someone alive. Only later have you the leisure to work on bettering the person's motivation or theology.
2. The person contacted you for a reason. Diplomacy and warmth may maintain that contact; hope and caring may forestall a suicide attempt.
3. Any threat of suicide ought to be taken seriously.
4. You didn't cause the person's problems, and you may not be able to fix them. Your responsibility is to try to help; you cannot be held responsible to succeed. The person may die.

Things to do or say:
1. Keep the person talking. It's hard for him or her to talk to you and follow through on suicide plans.

2. Show love, compassion, concern, respect; absorb anger, accusations, bitterness, manipulation.
3. Defuse the suicide plan if possible. Have the person flush drugs down the toilet, unload or dismantle a firearm, seek company, promise to call you before doing anything rash, etc.
4. Offer better options than suicide. You can probably see many where the caller sees none.
5. Remember to pray the person to safety, too.

Things not to do or say:
1. Do not make light of the situation. This threat could be a final try for help, even if it appears far-fetched.
2. Do not load on guilt over thoughts of suicide. Most suicidal people carry a heavy load already.
3. Do not leave the person alone. A relative, friend, neighbor, or fellow church member needs to remain with him or her.
4. Do not allow your anxiety to show. The caller needs a calm, controlled, capable presence to counter his or her emotional imbalance.

For further study:

Baker, Don, and Emery Nester. *Depression: Finding Hope and Meaning in Life's Darkest Shadow*. Portland, Oreg.: Multnomah Press, 1983.

Collins, Gary. *How to Be a People Helper*. Ventura, Cal.: Vision House, 1976.

Hart, Archibald. *Counseling the Depressed*. Waco, Tex.: Word Books, 1987.

Lum, Doman. *Responding to Suicidal Crisis*. Grand Rapids, Mich.: William B. Eerdmans Publishing Co., 1974.

Pretzel, Paul. *Understanding and Counseling the Suicidal Person*. Nashville: Abingdon, 1972.

ELEVEN

ALCOHOL AND DRUG PROBLEMS

Never, never, never forget that we are different. We cannot live like others. Our difference is this: We cannot drink alcohol.

AN ALCOHOLIC

One of my earliest memories of comedy involved an aging vaudevillian named Mr. Pastry. With amazing dexterity and comic timing, Mr. Pastry performed "The Passing-Out Ceremony" on "The Ed Sullivan Show." While music played, Mr. Pastry acted out a group of men drinking, dancing, and cavorting until they passed out. Our family laughed and laughed at this act. On vacation we mimed our way to the resort dining hall, acting like a tipsy Mr. Pastry.

But when you think about it, drunkenness isn't all that funny. Consider these facts:

- An estimated ten million Americans suffer from alcoholism, about 4 percent of the population, one in twenty-five.

- If each of these has about four family members or close friends affected by that alcoholism, another forty million Americans are deeply affected (making fifty million, about one-fifth of our population, impacted heavily by alcoholism).

- One in ten social drinkers will become an alcoholic, and there is no way to predict accurately which one that will be.

- According to conservative estimates, about 6 percent of the work force is alcoholic, and they cost employers over fifteen billion dollars a year and contribute to a large proportion of work-related accidents.

● Heavy drinking contributes to an estimated 80 percent of fire and drowning accidents, 60 percent of violent crimes, and 30 percent of suicides.

● Someone dies because of drunken driving every twenty-two minutes.

● Alcoholism is our third-worst national health problem, following only cancer and heart disease.

Added to those cold facts are what pastors see up close: the countless individuals devastated, careers ruined, families split, children abused or neglected, potentials unreached, and hearts broken. This, anyone would call a crisis.

A Place of Help

Early in my pastoral career, I counseled a 45-year-old alcoholic. She was trying to dry out but having a rough go of it. I talked with Frances for hours, listening, being supportive, trying to arrange housing or a job for her, agreeing with her how bad things were, and basically patting her on the back saying she was doing the best she could.

Eventually she invited me to an Alcoholics Anonymous meeting. The meeting room appeared dark, the air was filled with smoke, and the table was surrounded by some rough-hewn characters, as well as others that looked like your ordinary man on the street. They went around the table introducing themselves by their first names and adding, "I am an alcoholic." When it got to me, I felt like saying, "I'm Jim, and I am out of place," but it didn't seem the place for humor.

I was wrong. Before the evening was out, I had laughed several times. I had also been amazed at the level of care and insight. A woman who looked like she'd seen it all seemed to know exactly what to say to a business-suited man crying about his last drunk. A craggy-faced man with a voice that sounded like he'd gargled with razor blades gave a testimony about how he'd given up his addiction to a "higher power" and how that had saved him from death.

But what really shocked me was how they treated Frances. I had been handling her problem with kid gloves; these fellow alcoholics put on the boxing gloves. She mentioned having "just a little drink now and then." They told her, "Honey, that's the stupidest thing you could possibly do. Why do you want to kill yourself?" She started crying when they didn't understand. They replied, "Ain't no one responsible for your drinking but you, so you have no reason to feel sorry for yourself." She stammered out that she couldn't help drinking sometimes. They responded, "Look, Baby, you have a sponsor, and you didn't call her. You could have, but you didn't. Don't give us any trash [they used a different word] about wanting to quit drinking. When you really want to quit, we'll be here. But until then, we don't want to hear your excuses."

This kind of verbal thrashing went on for some time, and I felt like jumping in to defend Frances. After all, we'd talked about her problems, and I could see why she resorted to the bottle, as much as I didn't like it. These folks, however, were jumping all over her. Couldn't they just be nice to her?

Finally they moved on to other people. Some they tenderly encouraged. Others they applauded. Still others they bashed harder than Francis. As she and I drove away from the meeting, I had to ask: "How could you stand the way they treated you?"

"They were right," Francis replied. "They knew I was making excuses. You can fool some people, and we alcoholics get pretty good at it, but it's hard to fool another alcoholic. They've been where I am, and they see right through my rationalizations. They told me tonight what they had to say, and I love them for it."

Francis, I learned, needed those Alcoholics Anonymous meetings as much as she needed food and shelter. They were her one lifeline to sobriety. The last time I saw her, she was holding down a good job and living free of alcohol. Alcoholics Anonymous was responsible. I had been only a nice crutch to help her continue drinking.

I learned something: For alcholics, AA is indispensable. Rare indeed is the alcoholic who can stay dry without it. Often the best thing I can do as a pastor is to get an alcoholic to attend Alcoholics Anonymous meetings.

They don't want to go. The typical excuses are threefold: (1) *I don't like the people there.* That usually translates: I'm too good for that crowd. They're nothing but alcoholic losers.

It's true that often there are some Dickensian characters, but groups also contain judges, bankers, merchants, churchgoers. Often there are several groups to choose from. Suggest that the alcoholic go to at least six meetings before deciding to drop a group. By that time, he should find the value greater than the discomfort.

(2) *They smoke too much, and the language isn't nice.* It's true that heavy smoking and sometimes coarse language do characterize many Alcoholics Anonymous meetings. The people there are working on the one most important problem in their life: addiction to alcohol. The other niceties come later.

A few nonsmoking groups are available, though, or people can find the best spot in the room to avoid smoke. Some groups cater specifically to Christians. But apart from that, the question remains: If you were on the Titanic, would you wait for a nonsmoking lifeboat with cultured people?

(3) *I don't have time.* Few people relish the addition of another meeting (or several) every week. But we do have time to do what is truly important, and AA meetings aren't only important; they're essential.

Alcoholics Anonymous is built around the Twelve Steps. They can be found in AA literature, and any member ought to be able to recite them. Here are the steps:

1. We admitted we were powerless over alcohol — that our lives had become unmanageable.

2. Came to believe that a Power greater than ourselves could restore us to sanity.

3. Made a decision to turn our will and our lives over to the care of God *as we understood Him.*

4. Made a searching and fearless moral inventory of ourselves.

5. Admitted to God, to ourselves, and to another human being the exact nature of our wrongs.

6. Were entirely ready to have God remove all these defects of character.

7. Humbly asked Him to remove our shortcomings.

8. Made a list of all persons we had harmed, and became willing to make amends to them all.

9. Made direct amends to such people wherever possible, except when to do so would injure them or others.

10. Continued to take personal inventory and when we were wrong promptly admitted it.

11. Sought through prayer and meditation to improve our conscious contact with God *as we understood Him*, praying only for knowledge of His will for us and the power to carry that out.

12. Having had a spiritual awakening as the result of these steps, we tried to carry this message to alcoholics, and to practice these principles in all our affairs.

(The steps are written purposely in vaguely religious language. The founders were Christians. Many of the present members are strongly Christian. The power of the twelve steps is God at work. However, in order to involve many people from a wide variety of backgrounds and beliefs, the language of the steps and the tone of the meetings remain nonsectarian.)

Printed there in black and white, the steps don't look all that powerful. But backed up with the tough love of fellow AA members, those twelve steps have revolutionized lives. Over a million people today are remaining sober for another day because of Alcoholics Anonymous. It works.

Alcoholics Anonymous reminds its members that no matter how long they've gone without alcohol, they are still alcoholics. That's why the introduction at every meeting: I'm so-and-so, and I'm an alcoholic. They know they cannot consume alcohol in any amount. They are only one drink away from addiction for the rest of their lives. Many continue to attend AA regularly throughout their lifetime. Even after long sobriety, they need the group, and the group needs them.

Confronting the Alcoholic

But the crisis of alcoholism often is that the alcoholic does not or will not seek help. How does a pastor drive an alcoholic into the arms of rescue?

Not alone. One of the most successful — and also problematic — ways to stir an alcoholic into seeking help is the *guided confrontation* or *intervention*. In an intervention, a small number of significant people in the alcoholic's life (spouse, children, employer, physician, best friend, etc.) lovingly but firmly confront the alcoholic with specific, undeniable evidence of his alcoholism and how it has hurt others.

When it works properly, a brief breach is knocked in the alcoholic's defenses, and for a moment he sees the destruction his alcoholism has caused. At that crucial point, the idea is to get the alcoholic to admit himself immediately into a thirty-day residential or outpatient treatment program, or to commit to attending ninety Alcoholics Anonymous meetings in as many days. One of these three options — inpatient treatment, outpatient care, or a megadose of Alcoholics Anonymous, in descending order of effectiveness — is the desired outcome of an intervention. Each option has been proven to make a significant impact on even reluctant alcoholics.

A guided confrontation is not something to be entered into lightly or without significant preparation. If it fails, the alcoholic can be harmed, and it isn't unknown for an angry alcoholic to threaten or pursue violence against the interveners. Therefore skilled professional help in the intervention is mandatory. Such qualified counselors can often be located through a local drug and alcohol council or by checking with Alcoholics Anonymous. Some medical societies have a local

"Impaired Physicians Committee" to help doctors with chemical dependencies, and they can recommend a physician with experience in interventions. The Johnson Institute (10700 Olson Memorial Highway, Minneapolis, MN 55441) pioneered this tactic and can give information about finding help. To repeat, don't try to do an intervention without preparation and training.

What does an intervention look like? Anderson Spickard, a physician and co-author with Barbara Thompson of *Dying for a Drink*, suggests in that book four preparatory steps:

1. Intercessory prayer. People cannot rescue an alcoholic, but God can. Prayers of surrender and intercession are more than a nice addition to the preparation. Spickard considers them mandatory.

2. Education. Those involved need to understand alcoholism. Misinformation and ignorance heighten the chance for a botched intervention.

3. A support group. Al-Anon is an Alcoholics Anonymous-related group for family members of alcoholics. At Al-Anon meetings spouses and children find support and understanding and the strength to make the hard choices to quit enabling the alcoholic.

4. The end of enablement. The family and other enablers need to let the alcoholic experience the consequences of his addiction. Says Spickard: "As long as he can drink *and* lead a reasonably normal life, he will drink. If suddenly he finds himself paying his own fines, cleaning up after himself when he is sick, making his own explanations to his boss, facing bankruptcy, and, if necessary, serving a jail sentence, then he begins to comprehend an important message from reality."

At the intervention itself, each of the members lovingly and dispassionately tells the alcoholic about specific, documented results of his drunkenness: a party ruined, a child disgraced in front of friends, the car being wrecked, creditors demanding these bills be paid, the time he broke the furniture in the basement. Two key participants are the family physician and the alcoholic's boss — the physician to document present and expected medical complications, and the boss to warn of indisputable employment ramifications. For an active church member, the pastor can be key. These people make the problem public. It is no longer a family secret.

A rehearsal should be held. Running through the scenario allows those emotionally involved to surface anger or sorrow and deal with it before the intervention. It also allows for tight scripting and timing. The intervention must be well planned.

A reservation for a treatment facility ought to be arranged for that day or the following one. Employment plans should be arranged for a leave of absence. All impediments to leaving immediately for the treatment need to be anticipated and taken care of. The idea is to capitalize on the vulnerable moment.

Some interventions only partially work. The alcoholic softens but won't go into a program. Often an adamant promise to quit by himself is the most the alcoholic will give. In that case, interveners seek a written and signed promise that at the first sign of alcohol consumption, the alcoholic will then commit himself to a care program.

If the intervention fails, it can be tried again. Time and negative circumstances may push the alcoholic across the line next time. If not, the family probably has been brought together by the intervention process, and they have the satisfaction of at least trying to hinder the course of their loved one's alcoholism.

Spouses of Alcoholics

According to Alexander C. De Jong, a pastor who was himself an alcoholic, in *Help and Hope for the Alcoholic*, "Ninety-seven percent of all alcoholics are persons raising families, holding jobs, struggling to do their best to function in the face of a killer disease." That means a lot of husbands, wives, and children are living with an alcoholic — and a lot of pain.

With all the difficulties of an alcoholic spouse — financial problems, social embarrassments, possible abuse, worry, lies and deception, assuming the alcoholic's responsibilities on top of one's own, psychological games playing — I sometimes wonder what holds such a marriage together. The answer is probably threefold: intermittent reinforcement, reciprocal roles, and, the best, *agape* love.

Alcoholics, like anyone, have their good sides. When sober, they can be charming, loyal, loving, highly competent, humorous, caring, chivalrous — all the good things people love in each other. These sober times dominate the relationship in the beginning. And even well into alcoholism, sober periods may predominate or at least punctuate the marriage, sometimes for extended periods. Psychologists call this *intermittent reinforcement,* and behavior that has been shaped by intermittent reinforcement is the hardest to extinguish. Even when the down times get more frequent and harder to take, the memory of the up times keeps alive the behavior of loving the spouse. And, who knows, maybe this time he really *will* stay sober and things will look up.

Reciprocal roles means that both the alcoholic and the enabler gain something from the arrangement. A husband who wants to dominate his wife can do so when she remains helplessly drunk. A wife with a need to rescue can continually mother her alcoholic husband and take care of him. People with poor self-images sometimes feel deep down that they don't deserve a "whole" spouse, so they settle for a spouse fractured by alcoholism.

Agape love is realistic and long-suffering. It loves in order to give worth to the beloved, not because of the beloved's worth. This kind of love can keep a marriage going long after most would give up on it. It can't be soft love that gives in to a spouse's alcoholism; it is a tough love that is willing to do whatever is necessary to bring about the best results for the spouse. That sometimes means believing in the spouse who cannot believe in himself. It often means bearing great hurt and coming back for more — on realistic, helpful terms. *Agape* love loves the alcoholic in spite of the alcoholism, but works to love the alcoholic through and *beyond* the alcoholism.

Sometimes love means leaving a spouse. It may be to prove dramatically the gravity of the alcohol addiction, or it may be because of the welfare — physical, emotional, and/or financial — of the sober spouse and children. Whether that leaving means separation or divorce is something each spouse and each pastor have to consider.

In any case, the spouse will need the understanding and support of a congregation. Spouses in many ways need the same kind of Christian warmth and understanding they would require if the alcoholic were lost to death. They have to learn how to grieve the loss, at least temporarily, of a loved one.

Besides counsel and warm support, the best thing a pastor can do for the spouse of an alcoholic is to connect him or her with Al-Anon. These people have been through or are going through what this spouse is experiencing.

Children of Alcoholics

Spickard lists four classic ways children defend against the troubles of a parent's alcoholism:

The family hero. Some kids attempt to pick up every ball an alcoholic parent drops. They become old and responsible years before their time. They compulsively try to fix everything in the family and eventually become frantic when more things fall apart than they can handle. These children often do very well in school and appear to be model kids. Unfortunately, they pay a price by being practically unable to let up. Some in their thirties or forties simply fall apart from the strain.

The placater-servant. This child takes responsibility for everything. Well attuned to the slightest hurt or disagreement, this child steps in to try to smooth feelings. Self-esteem is gained by how much this child gives of himself or herself. Sometimes this one becomes the family clown in an attempt to ease tension.

The adjuster. This child vanishes into the woodwork. He

figures if he can just stay out of trouble's way, things will be okay. He makes no waves, casts no shadow. He's the one no one remembers at class reunions, and enters life ill prepared for responsibilities. Emotional detachment and apathy helped him through a difficult family life but sabotage his chances as an adult.

The rebellious child. She acts out her problems to get attention, for even negative attention is better than no attention. This child is often prone to abuse drugs and alcohol and enters adulthood on the way to trouble — if not squarely enmeshed in it.

These children need help, and lots of it. Spickard writes, "The passage of time seldom heals the wounds of children of alcoholics. Unless they get help for their deep psychological and spiritual difficulties, for the remainder of their lives they will be at high risk for the development of addiction or emotional collapse. And chances are they will pass these problems on to their children and grandchildren. . . ." By helping them obtain help, a caring pastor and congregation can see that these children don't fall through the cracks of society.

Drug Abuse

Much of what has preceded can apply to drug abuse. The substance differs, and some medical implications vary, but the result is the same: addiction to a substance that promises relief and offers only progressive pain.

I recently asked a pastor of an affluent suburban church about his involvement with parishioners with drug problems. His immediate response was, "I haven't had much experience with that." But then he started remembering, and right away instances came to mind. Drugs are everywhere.

One time Ben (what I'll call the pastor) got a call from a young woman named Jackie. Her boyfriend, Andy, had been an elder in the church. Andy was in his late thirties, divorced, the father of a couple of young kids. He was a top-notch businessman on the fast track to wealth and success. Jackie had bad news: "Andy is on cocaine. I know I don't go to your church, but Andy does, and he thinks a lot of you and Ginny [Ben's wife]. I need you to help me help Andy."

As they talked, the idea of an intervention came up, but Ben realized he had no experience in that sort of thing. Jackie was willing to give it a try, so she and Ben and Ginny went to a nearby hospital to get information. There they got the training they needed to attempt an intervention with Andy.

They scheduled a nice dinner at Jackie's house. After dinner, Ben spoke. "Andy, we have something to say to you. We love you, but we want you to get free of your cocaine habit." That startled Andy. He didn't know they knew. "You're a phony, Andy," Ben continued. "You're professing one thing and living another. Do you know how horrible you're making life for your kids? Do you have any idea of the hurt you're bringing them?" Ben hit hard.

Then Jackie began. "Andy, I really care for you, but your cocaine is ruining our relationship. Do you realize that three times in the last month you've stood me up? I know what you were doing. It was your cocaine. We will not be able to continue our relationship if you keep your cocaine. Andy, it's either cocaine or me. You've got to make a choice."

Then came Ginny's turn. Ginny was special to Andy, like a second mom. Her job was to soften up a little: "Andy, I don't know what to say. I guess I just feel betrayed by you. I so respect you that it's hard to think of you throwing your life away to cocaine."

Andy sat a little dazed. He didn't say much. "He was like a dog with his tail between his legs that night," Ben remembers.

Soon afterward, Ben and Andy's eldest daughter, a 12-year-old, met with him. She pleaded with her dad, "You've got a cocaine problem. You need help. We want you to go to a hospital where you can get straightened out." Andy wavered, but he wouldn't yield that much. He was determined "to do it on my own," but agreed to see a counselor Ben recommended.

He started doing well for a while, but a day came when he

was to take Ben and Ginny to a Cubs game. When he showed up forty-five minutes late, they suspected something was wrong. They knew it once they were with him. He broke down and confessed to Ginny, and Ben and Ginny had to tell his counselor.

Again Andy was back on the road to recovery. He's still getting excellent care from a counselor. Ben believes Andy's going to make it this time. The counselor once told Ben, "If it weren't for the church, we would have lost Andy."

Ben had heard that after the dinner confrontation, Andy had told a friend how angry he was at Ben and Jackie — somehow Ginny had been spared the anger. Ben had worried about risking the relationship, but he decided it was worth it to save Andy. What good would the relationship be if Andy were lost?

"I didn't want to be judgmental," says Ben, "but the time does come to not pull your punches. That's why I came across so tough with him at that dinner confrontation. Those were things he needed to know — in the context of my regard for him. And you'll notice I didn't carry the load myself. I gathered others around me. Problems of addiction are too taxing to try to carry alone. I'm thankful for a church that stands with me in times of crisis."

As it turned out, both the relationship and Andy were retained. He stayed in the church, the men's group surrounded him with support, and his life is fitting back together.

But a caution comes from Ed Gouedy, pastor of First Presbyterian Church in Fort Thomas, Kentucky: "With cases of substance abuse, so often the problem is not over when it's over. Recidivism rates are discouraging. The power of evil is incredible, and sometimes you feel like you're running the same bases over and over again. But the power of the Holy Spirit to change the 'incorrigible' never ceases to amaze me, either."

Quickscan
ALCOHOL AND DRUG PROBLEMS

Immediate concerns:
1. Drugs and alcohol can be toxic — deadly. Obtain immediate emergency medical aid if any indication of a drug overdose or an alcoholic coma is evident. A fifth of alcohol ingested in an hour can kill.
2. People high on drugs or drunk on alcohol can be violent and dangerous. Do not attempt to restrain them unless heroic efforts are called for.
3. You cannot reason with a drunk. Get medical help and talk later when the drunk is sober.

Keep in mind:
1. An alcoholic will probably be able to outtalk you with denial and rationalization. Reason will not sway the alcohol addict; the pain of consequences may.
2. Unless the benefits of sobriety appear significantly stronger than the benefits of alcohol or drugs, the addict will not give up the addiction. The most humane treatment is to expose the addict fully to the personal and family pain he is causing.
3. The addict cannot quit no matter how strong his will. Until he realizes he is helpless, he will resolutely pursue dead ends.
4. Addiction affects a family system. The whole family often needs help.
5. The single most effective way to help is to convince the addict to enroll in a thirty-day in-patient treatment program based on Alcoholics Anonymous guidelines. Out-patient programs or ninety Alcoholics Anonymous meetings in as many days are other alternatives.

Things to do or say:
1. Provide love, encouragement, and support without sheltering the addict from consequences of his actions.

2. Suggest, urge, *shanghai* the person to go to Alcoholics Anonymous or Narcotics Anonymous meetings.
3. Counsel and obtain help for family members affected by an addicted member.
4. Help loved ones arrange for an intervention led by competent and experienced professionals.
5. Provide literature and help educate everyone involved about the realities of drug and alcohol addiction.

Things not to do or say:
1. Do not use guilt, especially with Christian addicts. They feel great guilt already, even if not spoken, and further guilt without release pushes them toward suicide.
2. Do not become an enabler. Let them bear the consequences of their actions. Crises can actually be good, *if* the addicts have to mop up the consequences themselves.
3. Do not expect an alcoholic to quit by will power. An addict is powerless over his addiction. God must intervene.
4. Do not be too hard on yourself if your efforts seem wasted. You cannot rescue someone. God can, and he may use you. And he may not. That's up to him.

For further study:
Alcoholics Anonymous. 3d ed. New York: World Services, Inc., 1976.
DeJong, Alexander C. *Help and Hope for the Alcoholic.* Carol Stream, Ill.: Tyndale House Publishers, 1982.
Johnson, Vernon E. *I'll Quit Tomorrow.* New York: Harper & Row, 1980.
Spickard, Anderson, M.D., and Barbara R. Thompson. *Dying for a Drink: What You Should Know about Alcoholism.* Waco, Tex.: Word Books, 1985.

Alcoholics Anonymous World Services, Inc.
Box 459 Grand Central Station
New York, NY 10163

Al-Anon
A.F.G., Inc.
P.O. Box 182
Madison Square Station
New York, NY 10159-0182

The Johnson Institute
10700 Olson Memorial Highway
Minneapolis, MN 55441

National Council on Alcoholism
733 Third Avenue
New York, NY 10017

TWELVE

BEYOND CRISIS

A misty morning does not signify a cloudy day.

ANONYMOUS

I received an amazing call the other night. It was from Cory.

You'll remember I began this book with the story of Cory, the one whose family had pushed her out of the home onto emotional "black ice." For over eleven years I'd heard nothing from her. I'd assumed she had died of amyotrophic lateral sclerosis, the terminal disease she had the last time I saw her, blind and deaf, in a hospital.

As I wrote the chapter, however, I thought of another pastor who knew her. I called him to talk over what he remembered of Cory, and he surprised me with an address where he thought she might be living. I wrote, and Cory called a few days later.

Cory is doing great!

She eventually left that Burbank hospital in which I last saw her. Her eyesight and hearing had returned, and she had regained some use of her limbs. She set up life in a studio apartment with a visiting nurse to help her. But although she was determined to make it, she didn't. Her disease, which turned out to be multiple sclerosis, a debilitating disorder but not nearly as life threatening as ALS, struck again with a vengeance. She was placed in a nursing home.

For over a year she lived as the only young person among worn-out and senile residents. She felt terribly alone. "There is scarcely a way to describe the despair of gathering darkness in a convalescent home," she says, "hearing the moans of the gloomy and the forgotten, listening to the weeping in neighboring rooms, and having one's lifeless arms and legs being bathed by girls my age who had Thanksgiving or Christmas plans at the end of the evening. I loathed self-pity, but during those endless nights I often wondered, *Is this how it's going to be forever?*"

She lost her sight again, and her limbs failed to the point she couldn't walk or even feed herself. Her spinal column played nasty tricks on her brain, sending signals that her body was on fire. The pain was so excruciating that her doctor kept her on morphine. People would call on her a couple of times, but only one or two continued. It was too difficult to see her in that state; they couldn't take it.

But with the help of a couple of people who wouldn't let go, Cory dug deep one more time and began to fight her crisis. "When my sight returned after one episode, I'd look out the windows," she recalls. "I'd picture myself as one of the many birds I could barely see circling the hospital roof. Symbolically, I became that bird. In my mind, it was going to take a belief almost equal to believing I could fly to keep me from spending the rest of my life in my bed. The birds, in their soaring and enviable freedom, always seemed to say, 'Hey! Look at us! We don't know how we do it, but *we are flying!*' Of course, I knew who was responsible for their flight. So every day, likewise, I *believed* I would walk, which was on an equal level to flight in my realm. Then, eventually I was saying, 'Hey, look at me. *I am walking!*'"

Cory never gave up, and Someone else didn't give up on Cory. "Somewhere in all my messing around," Cory says, "amid all the games playing with people and with him, I started thinking about God. It was like he was a strict dad, and I was a kid full of mischief — you know, snitching food from the table, teasing other kids, being a real pain. And every once in a while, I'd look over at him to see how he was responding. Finally it was as if that Father said, 'That's enough!'

"I had pushed as far as I could, and now I found the limit. It amazes me that he's so patient. I think I was tired of messing around with God, too. So we had a big talk — God and I — and we came out of it with a whole new relationship."

Cory amazed the medical people working with her. Out of compassion, they'd wanted her to face the reality that she'd be institutionalized the rest of her life. She told them she'd walk again, and what's more, she'd leave that nursing home!

She did it. Her MS eased, as it sometimes does, and one day she emerged a victor. "I walked out that front door and smelled the fresh air for the first time in months," she recalls, "and I knew I was free! I'd been hurt, and I'd be hurt again, but life goes on. I told God, 'Now I know you're really there!' There's nothing in the whole world you can't handle once you have that relationship and start seeing how he has sustained you all along."

Cory got another place to live, found a job, received a grant, and returned to college. She became part of a church. Before long, she almost miraculously received custody of a baby girl. That baby gave her renewed spark. She was proud of being able to give her the proper care. "There were times when I wheeled my wheel chair around a college lab with a baby in my lap," she laughs.

Within a couple of years she met and married a remarkable man who had lost his first wife to multiple sclerosis after several years of tenderly nursing her. He and Cory legally adopted the little girl, and since then they've added a baby boy to their family. They've been married six years now, living a regular life, attending church, having the normal ups and downs any family does. I'm thrilled for her.

As Cory reflected on her life, she said softly, "It's scary being vulnerable. As I look back on all that happened to me and how I scraped through it, at this point it's almost like reading an interesting script. Sometimes I wonder, *Who* was *that girl?* Well, at least the script had a happy ending."

Indeed, it does. Cory draws an analogy between parenting and crisis counseling: "When my son comes up to me crying and upset, I pick him up, hold him in my arms, give him hugs, and kiss his scraped knee or hurt finger. Any parent knows how many times you have to do that while raising a child. I doubt if he'll remember each time I pick him up like that, but he'll probably remember the fact that I did it. That's what he'll hold on to. That's what will get him through the difficult times — a whole pattern of loving attention."

Then Cory made my day — no, my decade. "That's what you did for me when I was down. You let me know things would work out. That made the difference when I was wavering between watching (quite literally) for the light of day to arrive or throwing everything aside to wait for the end to come. I will always remember how faithfully you were there, an extension of God's arms. That's what I have to thank you for."

And that's why we're called into crisis.